C000244838

The FT guide to managing your money

In an increasingly competitive world, we believe it's quality of thinking that gives you the edge – an idea that opens new doors, a technique that solves a problem, or an insight that simply makes sense of it all. The more you know, the smarter and faster you can go.

That's why we work with the best minds in business and finance to bring cutting-edge thinking and best learning practice to a global market.

Under a range of leading imprints, including *Financial Times Prentice Hall*, we create world-class print publications and electronic products bringing our readers knowledge, skills and understanding, which can be applied whether studying or at work.

To find out more about Pearson Education publications, or tell us about the books you'd like to find, you can visit us at **www.pearsoned.co.uk**

The FT guide to managing your money

How to be better off by making better financial decisions

Cliff D'Arcy

FT Prentice Hall
FINANCIAL TIMES

An imprint of Pearson Education
London ▪ New York ▪ San Francisco ▪ Toronto ▪ Sydney ▪ Tokyo ▪ Singapore
Hong Kong ▪ Cape Town ▪ Madrid ▪ Paris ▪ Milan ▪ Munich ▪ Amsterdam

PEARSON EDUCATION LIMITED

Edinburgh Gate
Harlow CM20 2JE
Tel: +44 (0)1279 623623
Fax: +44 (0)1279 431059
Website: www.pearsoned.co.uk

First published in Great Britain in 2009

© Pearson Education Limited 2009

The right of Cliff D'Arcy to be identified as author of this work has been asserted
by him in accordance with the Copyright, Designs and Patents Act 1988.

ISBN: 978-0-273-71703-4

British Library Cataloguing in Publication Data
A catalogue record for this book can be obtained from the British Library

Library of Congress Cataloging in Publication Data
A catalog record for this book is available from the Library of Congress

All rights reserved. No part of this publication may be reproduced, stored in a
retrieval system, or transmitted in any form or by any means, electronic,
mechanical, photocopying, recording or otherwise, without either the prior
written permission of the publisher or a licence permitting restricted copying in
the United Kingdom issued by the Copyright Licensing Agency Ltd, Saffron
House, 6–10 Kirby Street, London EC1N 8TS. This book may not be lent, resold,
hired out or otherwise disposed of by way of trade in any form of binding or cover
other than that in which it is published, without the prior consent of the
Publishers.

10 9 8 7 6 5 4 3 2 1
13 12 11 10 09

Typeset in Stone Serif by 3
Printed by Ashford Colour Press Ltd, Gosport

The publisher's policy is to use paper manufactured from sustainable forests.

Contents

This book is dedicated to my late grandfather, Desmond, whose good sense inspires me always.

Acknowledgements

I'd like to offer particular thanks to Liz Gooster, my editor at Pearson Group, whose kind support and expert advice transformed this book from dream into reality. The same goes for her assistant, Martina O'Sullivan, and everyone else who generously spent time proof-reading and correcting my manuscript.

Also, I'm indebted to Ed Bowsher and Stuart Watson, the current and previous editors of *www.fool.co.uk*. My career as a financial writer began in 2003 with *The Motley Fool* and continues today. I am extremely grateful to its staff, readers and discussion-board posters for their support, suggestions and ideas.

I will applaud two more financial websites, both of which provide invaluable advice on personal finance. The first is my friend Martin Lewis's *www.moneysavingexpert.com*, which provides a deep mine of everyday advice on boosting the power of your pound. The second, *www.headlinemoney.co.uk*, hosts a superb library of information for financial writers.

Finally, I'd like to thank my parents, wife and children for helping me with the most important lessons in life – none of which are financial!

Cliff D'Arcy
Freelance Personal Finance Writer
July 2008

An introduction to managing money

How do you feel about your finances?

When you stop to think about your money, how does it make you feel? Do you feel in control, but would like to make your money work even harder? Do you feel nervous and wish for a better grip on your spending habits? Do you get a headache as soon as you start thinking about money? Or are you a total 'financial ostrich' with your head buried in the sand, too afraid even to open your bank statements?

Whichever of these groups you belong to, this book can help. In fact, it could turn out to be the most valuable book you ever buy! In eight lively, easy-to-read chapters, I show you how to get to grips with the key, everyday aspects of personal finance. The simple tools you pick up along the way will help you to approach money management with a new-found confidence. What's more, they will help you to improve your financial decisions, making you better off today and in the future.

Although this journey may seem a little scary, don't be put off – even if you've had money struggles before. I promise that learning to master your money really isn't that difficult to do. In fact, once you've got the hang of it, then things start to tick over nicely. At this stage, you can devote less time to money matters and more time to enjoying life. What's more, the pay-off can be *huge*, so it's worth sticking to your plan. With this book as your guide, you can confidently navigate the money-management maze!

Take back control of your life

If you want to feel more secure about your financial future, but don't want to spend too much time managing your money, then read on. Likewise, if your money is in a muddle and you yearn to be on top of your spending, borrowing and saving, then this book is for you. When it comes to money mastery, a little knowledge, together with a few handy rules and some clear goals go a long way.

As your friendly 'guide', my goal is to show you how to seize control of your money, making it your servant rather than your master. No matter how much or how little you have to spare, better management of what you do have will always produce worthwhile rewards. By creating your own personal and practical approach to money management, you can cut through all the chaos and confusion. In no time at all, you'll be in control of your money – and your life – for good.

A cure for the credit crunch

Financial wisdom has always been admired, and never more so than today, where overspending, record personal debts and high house prices cause headaches for millions of us. Indeed, according to a 2006 survey of users of 'how to' website, *www.videojug.com*, the skill that Britons would most like to acquire is how to make money.

Unfortunately, over the past three decades, the financial world has evolved to become impossibly complex. At the same time, financial education has been neglected by parents and teachers, leaving tens of millions of adults unable to manage and grow their money. Furthermore, thanks to the World Wide Web, there's vastly too much information out there.

For example, something as simple as choosing a savings account now involves trawling through more than *four thousand* different contenders in order to choose the ideal home for your spare cash! In the words of *Dilbert* creator, Scott Adams, 'information is pouring into our brains like a fire hose being directed at a teacup'. Is it any wonder that so many of us have given up hope of mastering our day-to-day money management?

This book aims to tackle this shortfall head-on, giving people the much needed skills-to-pay-the-bills. As debt problems soar, house prices dive and credit becomes more expensive and difficult to get, this book is the perfect cure for the credit crunch, as well as an antidote to hard times.

What will this FT Guide do for you?

This book explains – in simple, jargon-free language – how to turn money into your servant, rather than your master. It will help you to be, if not a 'Master of the Universe', then at least a master of your own finances. It will also show you how to manage your money as painlessly and easily as possible. What's more, it demystifies the world of money, providing you with practical advice on how to manage your personal finances. In other words, it makes your money work harder – with a little effort on your part, of course!

In eight easy-to-follow chapters, you will learn the simple secrets of financial success, including how to:

- increase the amount of money coming in, while reducing the amount going out;
- borrow money while handing over as little interest as possible;
- buy a home without putting a strain on your finances;
- create more cash from your savings;
- protect yourself and all that's important to you;
- build wealth over the years through investing;
- retire happily by planning ahead; and
- make sure that no swindlers steal your hard-earned stash!

Why listen to me?

Before becoming a financial writer in 2003, I spent 16 years in financial services, working for several of the UK's largest banks and insurance companies. During my time on the 'dark side', I spent 10 years practising the foul art of marketing. So, long before 'talking the talk', I was 'walking the walk'.

However, during the Eighties and Nineties, thanks to massive overspending, I managed to get my finances into a right mess. When I came close to throwing in the towel, I owed nearly £50,000 across 13 credit cards and three personal loans. Happily, over the past 10 years, I've 'turned the tanker around'.

❝ these days, instead of paying interest to banks, I earn it ❞

These days, instead of paying interest to banks, I earn it. Instead of working to make someone else rich, I make a good living – several times the average wage – from running my small businesses. Instead of being massively in debt and struggling to keep afloat, I have plenty of cash and a large portfolio of shares.

It's been said that 'men in mansions don't take advice from men in mud huts'. Today, my life is infinitely better and bears no resemblance to how it was a decade ago. Over the coming pages, I aim to teach you the lessons that I had to learn myself – often painfully!

A tip to get you started: the 'three Ps'

Before we leap into the first chapter, I'd like to give you an opening idea – one which will help to make the task ahead much easier. It may surprise you to learn that you only need get to grips with three fundamental things in order to gain control of your finances. You need to develop what I call your 'three Ps', as follows:

1   Your **personal philosophy**. Your understanding of – and attitude towards – money is unique. Thus, your money mindset is based on your own personal experiences. This is

why no two people behave alike when it comes to making and managing money.

2   Your **plan**. As arch-strategist Niccolò Machiavelli remarked around 500 years ago, 'Make no small plans, for they have no power to move the soul.' So, it is vital to set out your financial goals for the future – and to aim high!

3   Your **products**. Once you've decided on what you want from money and how you are going to get it, then you need some tools to do the job for you. This is where things get a bit more complicated, because you're now up against the dark arts of financial services marketing. (So, expect to be bombarded with mumbo-jumbo while you sift through thousands of products to find the best deals to suit your needs. But don't worry, because this book will be your guide, enabling you to cut through the red tape and discover what you really need to put your finances on track.)

Once you've run through – either mentally or, better still, on paper – your personal 'three Ps', then you can move on to absorb and act on the eight core chapters of this book. Let's look at the three Ps in little more detail before moving on.

Your personal philosophy

For some people, this is the most difficult aspect of the money-management process. This is because it forces you to weigh up what is most important to you in life. For example, you may have been taught to be penny-wise by prudent relatives, and therefore go through life in a thrifty fashion. On the other hand, you may be taking a different tack by boldly 'living for today', spending tomorrow's money and building up debts.

If you are determined to become a master (or mistress) of money, then you need to decide which side of this particular divide you want to lie. There's no point in kidding yourself that you're going to be a steadfast saver if you then repeatedly splurge all of your cash long before the next payday. In short, developing your money philosophy is about identifying your core *beliefs, habits* and *behaviours*. You then go on to explore how these govern your day-to-day financial affairs.

> ❝ think of yourself as an editor, whose job it is to root out bad habits ❞

Of course, your goal is to wipe out your worst habits and replace them with routines which increase your chances of financial success. Think of yourself as an editor, whose job it is to root out bad habits and improve your approach to money.

It might be useful to write down which behaviours cause you financial discomfort. Alongside these, you can come up with more rewarding replacements, such as these seven suggestions:

A problem behaviour	… and one possible alternative
Worrying about how much I've squandered during my latest spending spree	Learning to curb my consumer instincts, and get big discounts, by shrewdly shopping around
Spending too much on my credit card when I go out socially	Taking a limited amount of cash with me, so that I don't bust my budget each week
Paying hefty fines for allowing my current account to slip overdrawn without permission	Monitoring my bank account more closely so that I avoid these mishaps; arranging a cheaper approved overdraft
Being wary of opening bank and credit-card statements because I'm afraid of bad news	Putting in place a plan to reduce my debts, first to a manageable level and then to zero
Being frightened of unexpected bills suddenly arriving	Having an emergency fund of savings to cope with life's little setbacks
Automatically renewing my insurance policies when they fall due	Shopping around for quality quotes in order to get the same level of protection for less cash
Pinning my hopes for a richer future on the National Lottery	Having a long-term plan to build and preserve my wealth

Now it's your turn. Take a piece of paper, divide it in two with a vertical line, and then start listing any financial habits which worry you. From here, it's a simple step to come up with one or more attractive alternatives. Remember, identifying a problem is the first step to solving it, so they say.

If you're stuck for ideas, then first write down your problem. Next, think about how a close friend or relative – someone whom you think is 'good with money' – would advise you to deal with your difficulty. If you're still stuck, then turn to the relevant chapter of this book and start reading. Pretty soon, the answer will come to you. Off you go!

Your plan

Again, the form and content of your plan will depend on your personal circumstances. For example, a recent university graduate may set his/her sights on paying off expensive student debts as quickly as possible. At the other end of the spectrum, a worker approaching retirement may conclude that maximising financial security after giving up work is a top priority.

In between, a couple may aim to increase their disposable income in order to save more and meet the pressing financial commitments of family life. Likewise, a young couple's main priority may be to save hard in order to raise a deposit for their first home. When it comes to financial plans, there are as many courses as there are horses!

As with all things, your financial plans are sure to be more successful if you write them down. Furthermore, they are far more likely to come to fruition if they are realistic, with sensible goals and timescales. For instance, there's no use planning to make a million over the next decade if you can't even find a spare £10 a month to save. So, by all means go for it with big, bold plans, but acknowledge that you need to take genuine steps to produce these outcomes.

Generally speaking, I've found that a plan works best when presented as a to-do list on paper or PC. Also, from my own experience, I've never had more than 10 steps in my 'financial staircase'. In fact, I tend to concentrate on my three top items, as otherwise there is a risk of spreading myself too thin.

Your products

When it comes to choosing financial products, you need to tread carefully, because it really is a minefield out there. Indeed, even when it comes to choosing something as apparently simple as a savings account, you have over 4,000 different offers to choose from.

Thus, the coming chapters are largely devoted to advice on identifying, searching for and sourcing the best tools for each job. Indeed, by the time you finish Chapter 8, you will have a sound idea of which products you need and where to find them. If you like, think of this book as your guide to navigating the vast financial maze that is financial services.

Now let's get to work by learning some helpful habits and better behaviours. We begin with the very foundation of good financial health: better budgeting and spending.

The benefits of better budgeting

In my view, budgeting is the absolute cornerstone of money management. After all, what chance do you have of building future financial security if you can't even balance your household budget from one month to the next?

Then again, budgeting is often regarded as a dull and tedious chore. This is not without good reason, as very few of us relish working through a bulky pile of paperwork and figures. Nevertheless, the reality is that budgeting is the core financial skill. Indeed, without gaining the ability to monitor and measure your money, you have no realistic possibility of managing and mastering it.

Managing your money is like driving a car

❝ making financial improvements is similar to progressing through the gears ❞

One way to think about your financial journey through life is to liken it to driving a car. Cars have different gears in order to overcome different challenges. For example, first gear is like an elephant, powerful and strong, and used for pulling away and climbing steep inclines. At the other end of the scale, top gear is like a cheetah, great for high-speed cruising, but don't try using it to drive off.

Thus, making financial improvements is similar to progressing through the gears of a gearbox. You need to make a good start, let the revs build, and then work your way through the gears. Get everything right and you can then flick on the cruise control, sit back and enjoy the road to riches!

Don't spend life stuck in first gear

At heart, budgeting is a very simple process and can be summed up by these two pieces of advice: *spend less than you earn* and *live below your means*. However, I've never found these two sayings to be particularly inspiring, so I prefer this more positive and exciting motto: *boost your income and batter your bills!*

To continue our motoring analogy, budgeting is (you guessed it) your first gear: without it, your journey can't even begin. So, no matter how humdrum it is, your first task is to find out exactly how much you have coming into and out of your household. You can then go about maximising your income and minimising your expenses. Ideally, this should leave you with a healthy surplus which you can use to improve your present or, even better, your future.

Once you've found first gear, then you can work your way through the gears, beginning by bashing your borrowing (Chapters 2 and 3). After this, you find third gear through saving (Chapter 4). Next comes fourth gear (protecting what's precious; Chapter 5) and things are really starting to build. After this, you hit top gear (investing and pensions; Chapters 6 and 7). Finally, you need to make sure that your car isn't stolen (scams; Chapter 8).

So, the first thing to do is to put your finances on a firm footing by finding first gear: budgeting. This is particularly crucial if you find yourself over-spending from month to month. Although you can do this for short periods in life, in the long term, you're driving up a dead end.

The basics of budgeting

First off, don't think of budgeting as a dull and lifeless task, otherwise it will become a burden rather than a benefit. Instead, think of budgeting as a really powerful tool which will help you to maximise your disposable income. No other process will do this for you, so budgeting is actually a pretty powerful device. Also, although the first few steps of budgeting can be pretty dreary, once you've taken them, then the future becomes much brighter.

To get your financial ducks in a row, your first step is to set aside some spare time. If you are incredibly organised, then you may need only an hour or two to get the ball rolling. However, if like me, you belong to the 'piling, not filing' school of organisation, then this initial process may take an entire morning or afternoon. For example, a day when it's pouring with rain would be a good time to stay indoors and sort out your finances.

Your first step to balance in your household budget is to track down every imaginable amount coming into and leaving your home. So, pull together your paperwork, even if it means working through a two-foot-high paper mountain filled with statements, payslips and so on. This job is done when you have a pile of documents showing all your monthly, quarterly and annual bills and sources of income. There, that wasn't too hard, was it?

(By the way, here's something to cheer you up. No matter how disorganised you may be, you're probably not in my league. After moving house in late 2007, my office/spare room was filled with boxes of assorted paperwork. Before my highly organised wife threw away 99% of my paper pile, it was almost the size of a garden shed. So, don't be embarrassed if you don't have a perfect grasp of your finances, because this precious gift is amazingly rare nowadays!)

Step two is to create a long list of all these sums, with money coming in listed in the first column and money going out in the second. While this can be done on paper, it's much easier to do so by creating and maintaining a spreadsheet in Microsoft Excel, or a free equivalent such as OpenOffice Calc.

Put it on your PC

By using a personal computer for budgeting, you can monitor
and measure your money much more easily, plus all the paperwork and calculations are done for you. In addition, most online
banking services allow you to download statements and transactions going back between three and 12 months, which saves you
having to re-key these figures. Furthermore, when your income
or outgoings change, it takes mere seconds to update your
spreadsheet.

The good news is that you don't need to create your own computerised 'statement of affairs', as this is already been done for
you by two barons of budgeting from The Motley Fool, see
www.makesenseofcards.com/soacalc.html. This spreadsheet can also
be used to monitor your assets and liabilities (in other words,
what you own and what you owe) when dealing with debt.

By entering your personal information in the boxes provided,
you have an instant 'photograph' of your household budget,
which can be saved, printed or posted for comments on a few
popular financial websites.

The BIG number: your disposable income

By subtracting your total outgoings from your total income, you
now know a key figure: your disposable income. Eureka!

With any luck, this number will be positive (that is, greater than
zero). However, your figure may be negative. This means that – in
common with millions of other Brits – you're spending more
than you earn. Nevertheless, the good news is that, unlike most
of us, you've finally got an idea of the size of your problem. The
rest of this chapter is devoted to helping you to head back into
the black.

On the other hand, you may find that you do indeed have
money to spare at the end of every month, perhaps because you
already have some useful financial skills. Well done, give yourself
a pat on the back. Then again, there's always room for improve-

ment, so you must still go through the process of boosting your revenue (earnings and other income) and trimming your expenses. Let's look at how you can do this:

Boost your earnings from work

One obvious way to get more income is to do more work. For example, if your present employer pays you for overtime or extra shifts, then a few extra hours each week could add hundreds of pounds to your annual salary. Likewise, when times are tough, there's nothing wrong with taking a second job, assuming your existing contract of employment doesn't forbid this.

❝ there's nothing wrong with taking a second job ❞

However, most part-time, evening and weekend work isn't terribly well paid. Have a look in your local papers and online for rates of pay in your area. You may find that most casual positions (such as in supermarkets, bars and restaurants) offer only the national minimum wage. From October 2008, this is £5.73 an hour for workers aged 22+.

Thus, you may find yourself earning under £4 an hour in a second job, after tax and National Insurance. This is unlikely to be as worthwhile as cutting back in other areas. For example, switching energy tariffs might take less than an hour, but save you, say, £150 a year. Also, all work and no play will raise your stress levels, so be sure to put aside some time for relaxation.

Check your tax and other deductions

One thing young workers quickly learn is that the starting figure (their gross pay) on their payslip is always a lot higher than the final figure (their net pay). In some cases, income tax, National Insurance contributions, pension payments and other deductions can gobble up to half of your wage.

It makes sense to check your deductions in order to make sure that the correct amounts are being subtracted. For example, HM

Revenue and Customs gets millions of tax bills and tax codes wrong every year. So, try the payslip checker at *www.digita.com/ taxcentral/home/employment/payslipcalculator/default.asp* and the tax code calculator at *www.taxcentral.co.uk/taxcentral/home/ employment/taxcodecalculator/default.asp*.

Claim benefits and other entitlements

One thing the government does very well is recycling our taxes back to us in the form of state benefits and other credits. However, some adults feel uneasy about dipping into the public purse. Nevertheless, by contributing to the upkeep of the country via our taxes, we become entitled to claim any and all benefits which the system sends our way.

Alas, the sheer number and variety of benefits available today make this system incredibly mysterious and difficult to navigate. There are benefits for people on a low income, families with children, carers, the disabled, unemployed people, the sick or injured, pensioners and the elderly. Then again, if you're childless, healthy and working then don't expect many benefits to come your way, because you're deemed not to need this safety net.

As the benefits system has grown and become more elaborate, more and more benefits are being means tested. In other words, you may qualify for these payouts if you meet certain criteria regarding your income, savings and working hours. Nevertheless, around nine out of 10 (90%) of the UK's 7.2 million families with children qualify for some form of state benefits or tax credits (although a significant proportion fail to claim these).

Here's a shortlist of widely available benefits:

- Child Benefit (a tax-free benefit paid to parents or guardians of children under 16 (20 if in further education);
- Child Tax Credit (paid to parents with income below a certain level);
- Working Tax Credit (paid to workers on a low income);

- Council Tax Benefit (help towards council-tax bills for tenants and homeowners);
- Housing Benefit (help towards rental costs for tenants);
- Pension Credit (a payment to pensioners whose income fails to reach a certain level).

As I said, the benefits system would tax a mind greater than Albert Einstein's, so you need expert help to navigate this maze. Try the free, independent advice website *www.entitledto.co.uk*, the official Benefit Enquiry Line on freephone 0800 882200, or the government advice at *www.direct.gov.uk/en/MoneyTaxAndBenefits/ BenefitsTaxCreditsAndOtherSupport/index.htm*.

Get a pay rise

As this book teaches you about money management and not careers advice, I won't go into too much detail here. However, from my personal experience, I do feel that it's worthwhile preparing your case in advance for an above-average pay rise. Although there is usually a fixed amount in a company's budget for pay rises, your job is to grab as large a slice of this pot as you can. After all, if you don't ask, then you don't get, so try creating a 'salary slide-show' to impress your boss!

Get help with childcare costs

After housing costs, childcare costs eat up a large part of working families' take-home pay. One way to reduce this cost is to sacrifice part of your salary in return for tax-free childcare vouchers from your employer. By doing so, you can claim up to £55 a week tax free, for a potential saving of up to £100 a month. For more information, visit *www.childcarevouchers.co.uk*.

Increase income from capital and investments

One way to increase your income is to boost the returns which you receive from income-generating assets, such as savings accounts, shares and so on. For instance, by switching your stash from a taxable savings account to a tax-free alternative, you could increase your savings interest by up to two-thirds (67%)! I reveal several of these tricks in Chapter 4 on savings and in Chapter 6 on investing.

Manage your money like a business (be CEO of 'Me plc')

One popular idea which originated in the USA is to regard your household as a business. Your job, therefore, is that of a chief executive officer whose aim is to maximise revenues while clamping down on costs. I quite like this approach, although partners could end up arguing over who becomes the CEO and who ends up as a common-or-garden director.

66 **maximise revenues while clamping down on costs** 99

Sell what you don't need

If I'm sure you'll agree that modern life is heavy with unnecessary items. For example, a search of your attic, garage or spare room will probably uncover lots of items for which you no longer have any use. To guide you, Arts and Crafts designer William Morris said, 'Have nothing in your homes that you do not know to be useful and believe to be beautiful.'

So, sift through this stuff and decide what you can't live without. The rest can be sold to the highest bidder, via car boot sales, advertising in local papers, eBay, Amazon Marketplace or wherever. Items easily sold include books, CDs, clothes, computers and software, DVDs, electrical equipment, jewellery, magazines, records, toys and videos.

Take in a lodger

You don't have to be a tycoon in order to make money from property. Indeed, under the government-approved Rent a Room scheme, you can let a room in your home to a lodger and earn up to £4250 a year, completely tax free. This comes to £81.73 a week, which would be a welcome boost to any tightly stretched budget. Of course, you don't have to have someone living with you all the time. Instead, you could let to short-term tenants, such as foreign students here during the summer months.

Bashing your bills and trimming everyday expenses

Now we've come up with a few ideas to boost your income, let's look at the other side of the budgeting coin: slashing your outgoings. In essence, there are three ways to do this:

1 Completely cut out spending on unnecessary or frivolous items.
2 Buy less of a particular item or service.
3 Pay less for what you must have (what I call 'gains without pain').

In other words, we're looking to buy less, pay less, or a combination of both. Here are some ideas to get you started

Be cautious at the cash machine

A decade ago, cash machines used to stock £5 and £10 notes. Nowadays, thanks to increased consumer spending, almost all cash machines stock £10 and £20 notes. In other words, you're forced to withdraw a tenner, even if you only need a fiver. So, you end up with more than you need and, frequently, this extra money being spent quickly. Hence, don't be too keen at the cash machine – only take out what you need and no more.

❝ only take out what you need ❞

(By the way, did you know that 'hole in the wall' and 'cashpoint' are trademarks of Barclays and Lloyds TSB respectively?)

Beware of your 'latte factors'

If your disposable income is a little too low for your liking, then you may need to 'sweat the small stuff'. In other words, you should identify and curb what Americans call your 'latte factors'. These are the little purchases which add up to substantial spending over time. For instance, with around 240 working days in a year, spending £5 on a coffee and croissant each workday adds up to £1200 a year!

Claim cashback

One way to earn as you spend is by getting cashback or points on your purchases. You can do this by using a cashback credit card (see Chapter 2), a supermarket loyalty card such as the Tesco Clubcard or the Nectar card, and by buying via one of the various cashback websites. For more information on cashback websites, go to *www.moneysavingexpert.com/shopping/cashback-websites*.

Don't keep up with the Joneses

We live in an era of conspicuous consumption, where neighbours and work colleagues compete to outdo each other on the image front. Many people refer to this money merry-go-round as 'keeping up with the Joneses'. Apparently, the Jones family act as some kind of benchmark for the lifestyle we all aspire to. However, given their excessive spending, I believe that the Joneses must be massively in debt by now. Thus, if you don't want to join them in a disastrous debt spiral, then don't give in to envy!

Get discounts on every major outlay

You'll notice that, so far, I have clearly failed to mention how to go about paying less for your everyday and major purchases. Naturally, it goes without saying that buying goods and services at lower cost (either by switching providers or securing discounts) is a fundamental part of bill-bashing.

However, I will not go into much detail about this topic in this book. That's because, when it comes to talking about getting more for less, money-saving expert Martin Lewis leaves everyone else for dead. As well as being the author of best-selling book *The Money Diet*, Martin runs the hugely popular *www.moneysaving-expert.com* website.

Frankly, this website is nothing short of magnificent, providing advice on saving on shopping and spending, utilities and communications, travel and transport, family and health, and all financial products. Anyone serious about switching and saving should join the millions of Brits who have signed up to receive Martin's weekly money-tips e-mail.

Another website which provides valuable advice on managing your money is The Motley Fool at *www.fool.co.uk*. Its daily e-mails provide a huge range of expert advice and guidance across the whole range of financial issues. Its weekly money-saving tips can be found at *www.fool.co.uk/money-saving-tips/money-saving-tips. aspx*.

Give to charity using Gift Aid

When you're feeling generous, think twice before throwing a coin or note into a collection box for a charity. By donating money via Gift Aid, the taxman also chips in on your behalf. For basic-rate taxpayers, Gift Aid turns a gift of £1 into £1.28, thanks to 22% tax relief. In addition, higher-rate taxpayers can reclaim 18% of this total via their tax returns, for a further saving of 23p. Thus, thanks to the joys of Gift Aid, a donation of £1.28 can cost as little as 77p. For more information, see *www.hmrc.gov.uk/ charities/gift-aid.htm*.

Haggle and shop around

Some people positively relish negotiating discounts by haggling with sales staff. For them, it's a bit like a tug of war, with the buyer wanting the lowest price and the seller the highest price. Some folk love to play suppliers off against each other, in order to take advantage of their rivalry. In my experience, merely asking for a discount and offering to pay cash will almost always yield a discount from the ticket price.

ff merely asking for a discount and offering to pay cash will almost always yield a discount jj

However, most adults don't like bargaining and prefer not to engage in the to-ing and fro-ing of haggling. Nevertheless, these people can still secure substantial discounts on their spending simply by using price-comparison websites. You may have heard of the popular general 'shopbots', such as *www.kelkoo.co.uk* and *www.pricerunner.co.uk*. However, there are also dozens of other price-comparison sites, including specialised searches for bargain books, CDs, DVDs and so on. You'll find a long list at *www.moneysavingexpert.com/shopping/cheap-online-shopping-shopbots*.

Keep a spending diary

When you make a financial transaction using a cheque, plastic card or other electronic system, this produces an easy-to-follow footprint in your financial records. Also, when using your debit card to withdraw cash, you should always get a receipt, in order to track your cash machine transactions. This allows you to monitor your spending and watch out for unusual or fraudulent transactions.

On the other hand, without receipts, it's very tricky to keep an eye on your cash spending. This is where a spending diary comes in handy. By recording all of your spending in a little notebook for, say, one month, you can build up an accurate record of where all your coins and notes go. This will give you an insight into your day-to-day spending that you won't get from looking at your bank statements.

Learn to love your bills

The majority of Britons would be unhappy to find a big pile of bills waiting on their doormat. Not me, because I've learnt to love my bills. After all, they show me how much I'm spending and act as a reminder to find lower tariffs. So, when an insurance renewal comes through the door, I see it as a call to shop around for a lower premium.

So, by keeping tabs on your bills, you gain a greater understanding of your overall expenditure. Then again, dealing with a big pile of bills is hardly exciting, especially if you have to spend time paying them all. That's why it's a good idea to put your bills on autopilot.

In other words, pay them by monthly, quarterly or yearly direct debit (DD) or standing order. Furthermore, over 100,000 organisations give discounts for paying by DD, because of the lower costs of this collection method. Paying by DD could save a typical household over £200 a year, according to *www.bacs.co.uk/BACS/ Consumers/Direct+Debit/Savings*.

Look at life's little luxuries

As well as identifying your latte factors, do broaden your spending search to look for more of life's little luxuries and treats. For example, could you live without:

- twice-weekly takeaways (£40 a week is more than £2000 a year)?
- smoking (20 cigarettes a day costs £2000+ a year)?
- your premium satellite television subscription, costing £600+ a year?
- your expensive gym membership (another £600 or so a year)?
- a daily newspaper (reading the paper's website could save you £200 a year)?

■ a £5 lunch each workday (taking a 'brown bag' lunch to work could save you £1000 a year)?

All of these things are 'would like to haves' instead of 'must haves'. If you're really struggling to make ends meet, then you must place priorities before luxuries!

You'll find more advice on living below your means at this very popular discussion board: *www.boards.fool.co.uk/Messages.asp? bid= 50074.*

Measure and manage your progress

It's important to remember that your budget is not static. Often, it will vary from month to month, thanks to variations in your bills and earnings. However, once you've set up your spreadsheet and done your filing, you need only a light touch on the wheel to keep driving your money management forward. Indeed, with the spadework out of the way, budgeting should require no more than 30 minutes a month. That's not too much to ask, is it?

What's more, thanks to inflation (rising prices), your outgoings will rise over time. Hence, it's important to put some padding into your budget or keep some savings in reserve. Also, you should adjust your budget figures when you get a pay rise or other extra money coming in. Likewise, when interest rates change and, for example, your mortgage repayments go up or down, your budget will need to take account of these variations.

In other words, your budget should not be a one-off snapshot, but a rolling film of your financial life.

Play your cards right

As I explain in Chapter 2, credit cards are incredibly useful tools. However, for those in debt, credit card problems can lead to sleepless nights. One nasty feature of credit cards is the minimum monthly repayment. Typically, this is a low percentage of the outstanding debt, say, between 2% and 3% of the balance.

The big problem here is that, as your debt reduces, so too does your minimum monthly repayment (because it's a fixed percentage of a falling amount). In effect, this prolongs the amount of time it takes to clear your balance, possibly leaving you in debt for decades. So, to bring forward your debt-free day, and to make budgeting easier, pay a fixed monthly amount onto your credit cards by direct debit or standing order.

The paradox of 'affluenza'

By improving your budgeting and spending, you can become a 'wiser miser' and learn lessons that will support you throughout the rest of your life. By going down this route to building wealth, you will find yourself in a much better position than, say, people who have suddenly come into money through an inheritance or windfall.

It is said that 'money doesn't buy happiness' and it's certainly the case that some wealthy people suffer from what psychologist Oliver James calls 'affluenza'. For some of us, the downside of material affluence and dog-eat-dog consumerism is anxiety, depression and other mental health problems. So, as your wealth grows, don't be seduced by the lure of fame, money, possessions, and physical and social appearance.Otherwise, you too could end up a victim of aggressive advertising, conspicuous consumption and 'selfish capitalism'.

One final word: keep it simple!

If you found money management difficult in the past, then this may be because you made things too complicated for yourself. The simpler your budgeting and spending become, the easier it will be to keep an eye on them. So, for instance, don't have four different current accounts when one Best Buy will do.

In time, and with the right preparation, you should be able to produce an at-a-glance guide to your personal finances. At this point, budgeting becomes a breeze. Won't that be a weight off your mind?

2

Becoming a better borrower

I n the first chapter of this book, we discussed how improving your budgeting and spending habits provide a welcome boost to your disposable income.

Then again, no matter how hard you work at managing your money, you're highly likely to turn to a lender at some point in your adult life. For example, most of us are forced to borrow in order to pay for major purchases such as homes and cars. In Chapter 3, we look at how to buy a home with the help of a mortgage. In this chapter, we focus on other kinds of borrowing, such as credit cards, overdrafts and personal loans.

The basic rule of borrowing is deceptively simple: *borrow as little as you can, for as short a time as possible, while keeping repayments affordable.* By going down this route, you pay the smallest amount of interest. However, this is easier said than done, especially when wages are being squeezed by increasing household bills and higher taxes.

Britons: the best borrowers in the world!

Sadly, when it comes to personal debt, we Brits now rule the world. By the end of July 2008, total personal debt (including mortgages) had reached a staggering £1448 billion (or £1.448

trillion). At this point, personal debt stood at 109% of GDP (gross domestic product), making Britons the most heavily indebted borrowers on the planet. Oops!

This debt mountain includes £1217 billion of domestic mortgages. However, in July 1996, total mortgage debt stood at £400 billion. As we discover in the next chapter, house prices tripled between 1996 and 2007. Therefore, it's hardly surprising that housing debt followed suit, trebling in less than 12 years.

As for the remaining £231 billion, this consists of unsecured (non-mortgage) debts, also known as consumer credit. In this category, we find everyday borrowing products such as current account overdrafts, car and personal loans, credit and store cards, and so on. With 48 million adults in the UK, the average unsecured debt comes to almost £4810 per person.

Thus, in the words of Errol Flynn, our inability to 'reconcile our net income with our gross habits' has led to a dramatic increase in unsecured lending since the mid-Nineties. In August 1996, the UK's non-mortgage debt came to less than £76 billion. By July 2008, it had more than tripled to £233 billion.

❝ our appetite for spending more than we earn is the underlying problem ❞

Thus, I think we can safely say that we Brits are indeed the world's best (or, in fact, the worst) borrowers. Nevertheless, it's important to note that the biggest borrowing binge in British history is merely a symptom. Our appetite for spending more than we earn is the underlying problem, and the reason why millions of us rely so heavily on credit to subsidise our lifestyle.

Military strategists say that in order to defeat an enemy, you must first understand him. Therefore, in order to dodge or destroy debt, you first need to learn all about it. Let's begin by looking at the most convenient and widely used form of borrowing: the humble credit card.

Credit cards

When it comes to credit cards, the UK suffers from 'plasticmania'. According to the banking payments group APACS, the UK has more credit cards than any other European country. The following facts from APACS demonstrate our affection for our 'flexible friends':

■ there are 67.3 million credit cards in issue in the UK;

■ more than six in 10 adults (62%) have one or more credit cards, a total of 30.8 million people;

■ in 2006, we spent over £133 billion on credit and charge cards; and

■ in 2007, we made 1.9 billion purchases on credit and charge cards.

In some ways, credit cards are like razor blades. When used correctly, they are simple, convenient tools which perform a useful task. However, when used recklessly, they can do considerable damage. Indeed, at their worst, they become WMDs: Weapons of Money Destruction!

So, play your cards right and you can enjoy all the benefits and convenience which credit cards have to offer. Then again, if you don't play by the rules, using a credit card can become extremely costly. Indeed, losing control of your plastic can cost you hundreds – or even thousands – of pounds a year. Thus, over the next few pages, you can learn how to make the most of your credit cards by becoming a card sharp.

The big problem with credit cards

As with most financial products, credit cards exist for one reason and one reason only: to make money for card issuers. They do this by charging fees and interest to cardholders, and by charging merchant fees to retailers. In other words, they exist to enrich bank shareholders, rather than to benefit the general public.

So, if you are to avoid all of the traps and pitfalls which lie in wait, then you need to know your enemy. Let's begin by looking at the biggest bill associated with credit cards: interest.

Interest

By July 2008, lending on credit cards had topped £55 billion, according to the Bank of England. Around three-quarters (75%) of this total is interest-bearing debt, so interest is charged on roughly £41 billion. Given that the average yearly interest rate on a credit card is around 16.5% APR (annual percentage rate), interest on credit cards is the thick end of £7 billion a year.

When quoting interest rates, credit card issuers always quote both a monthly rate and its annual equivalent, known as the annual percentage rate, or APR. Although these monthly interest rates may appear fairly modest, they can easily become unaffordable over long periods. Here's how to turn a monthly interest rate into its annual equivalent:

> Monthly interest rate: 1.5% (or 0.015)
> Add one: 1.015
> Multiply by itself 12 times*: 1.196
> Minus one: 0.1956
> Expressed as a percentage: 19.56%

Therefore, a monthly interest rate of 1.5% compounds over the course of a year into an annual interest rate of 19.56% APR. Likewise, 1% a month equals 12.68% APR, and 2% a month comes to 26.82% APR. As you can see, it pays to keep a close eye on your monthly interest rate, as small changes can make a big difference to your overall interest bill!

The best approach: be a full payer

Ideally, your goal should be to avoid paying any interest at all on your credit card. You can do this in different ways. The simple

*Mathematically, this is expressed as 1.015^{12}, where '^' means 'to the power of'.

way is to become a 'full payer' – someone who always pays off their monthly credit-card balance in full. The slightly more complicated way is to avoid interest by using 0% cards (see below).

In other words, the smart way to use credit cards is to use them to spend only what you can afford. By doing this, you ensure that you can always pay off your outstanding debt when your next monthly statement arrives. By using a credit card sensibly, you can enjoy interest-free credit, greater legal protection if suppliers fail to deliver or go bust and, in some cases, cashback as you spend.

Credit card statements work on a monthly cycle, on top of which you can enjoy between 14 and 28 days of interest-free credit. In total, this means that most credit cards provide you with between 45 and 59 days from your statement date until your payment date.

Thus, by setting up a monthly direct debit for your entire balance, you can ensure that your debt is cleared promptly each month. This disciplined approach will guarantee that you never pay a penny in interest, while enjoying almost two months of no-cost credit.

Interest-free (0%) credit cards and balance transfers

On Christmas Day 2000, the online bank Egg caused a sensation when it launched the UK's first 0% credit card for balance transfers. Egg's 0% credit card allowed new customers to transfer their existing card debts to an Egg Card and avoid paying interest on these balance transfers for six months.

Unsurprisingly, other credit card companies rushed to follow Egg's lead and, today, there can be as many as 100 different 0% cards to choose from. Over time, the 0% credit card market has evolved and changed as market competition has intensified. Today, it is possible to sign up for introductory 0% offers lasting between five and 15 months.

However, providing interest-free credit to new cardholders is a 'loss leader', because lenders lose money on these deals. In order to stem its losses, Barclaycard introduced a transfer fee in August 2005. Nowadays, all but a handful of 0% card issuers charge a balance-transfer fee. Typically, this fee amounts to between 2% and 3% of the value of each transfer. Thus, a balance transfer of £2500 would incur a fee of between £50 and £75.

When choosing a 0% balance-transfer card, you should check these four items before proceeding:

1 How long the 0% deal lasts – the longer, the better.
2 How high the transfer fee is.
3 Whether the 0% rate also applies to purchases and other spending (this is not usually the case).
4 The penalties for late or missed payments (£12 per offence is the norm).

You should also understand that a credit card issuer will not allow you to transfer balances between cards it issues. So, if you have a debt on a NatWest credit card, then you cannot transfer this debt to another card in the Royal Bank of Scotland group.

Also, you need to maintain a perfect payment history in order to hang onto your 0% deal. So, if you pay late, miss a payment or exceed your credit limit, then your 0% deal may be scrapped. Hence, it makes sense to set up a direct debit or standing order for at least your minimum monthly repayment.

Another bad move is to use a 0% balance-transfer card for everyday spending. Very few credit cards offer 0% interest on both balance transfers and retail spending. So, unless you're absolutely certain that you'll pay no interest on both purchases and transfers, then never take a 0% card shopping. Otherwise, you will most likely pay interest at standard rates on this spending, which is a big mistake. What's more, your repayments will go towards paying off your cheapest debt first, leaving your expensive debt lingering, possibly for years. You can learn more about this 'negative payment hierarchy' later in this chapter.

Finally, if you manage to play the 0% game well and enjoy several interest-free periods in a row, then congratulations. You are now a fully fledged 'rate tart'!

0% on purchases

Although not as popular as 0% balance-transfer cards, there is a growing number of '0% on purchases' credit cards. As you'd imagine, these allow you to spend while avoiding interest for an extended period. Typically, these cards give you a six to 12-month break from paying interest.

One way to use a 0% on purchases card to your advantage is to reduce your monthly repayments while increasing your savings. For example, let's assume that you spend £500 a month on your bog-standard credit card. As a full payer, you must find this sum every month in order to avoid interest.

By switching your purchases to a 0% on purchases card, you can avoid paying interest on your spending for, say, up to 12 months. As you're not paying interest for a year, you can set up a direct debit for your minimum monthly repayment. Typically, this will be between 2% and 3% of your outstanding balance.

Thus, after one month of spending, your repayment could be as low as £10. The remaining £490 can be deposited in a high-interest savings account in order to earn you extra interest. Just before your 0% deal comes to an end, you withdraw this cash pot and use it to repay your entire card balance. As a result, you have enjoyed interest-free credit for almost a year, paid much lower monthly repayments, and earned extra savings interest.

Of course, in order to take full advantage of these 0% offers, you need to be highly organised and very disciplined. Don't spend the spare cash in your savings account, and be sure to repay your card balance in full just before your 0% offer comes to an end. Otherwise, you'll start paying interest at the standard rate (probably 16%+ a year), which will eat into the profit from your extra savings interest.

It's worth noting that the most attractive 0% deals apply to both balance transfers and retail spending. However, 0% deals never apply to cash obtained by using your credit card in an ATM or withdrawing cash 'over the counter' (see below).

Now that we've covered the basics of credit cards, it's time to look at them in detail, with an A–Z of plastic.

Affinity and charity cards

There are over 1300 differently branded credit cards in issue in the UK. The majority of these are issued by seven big banking groups: Barclaycard, Capital One, Co-operative Bank, Halifax/Bank of Scotland, HSBC, MBNA and Royal Bank of Scotland.

While many of these credit cards are instantly recognisable, there are also hundreds of lesser-known 'affinity' and charity cards from which to choose. Many charities, professional bodies, sports clubs and unions have joined forces with leading credit card providers in order to issue their own branded cards.

One attraction of affinity cards is that they provide financial donations to a good cause or sports team. However, few affinity or charity cards make it into the Best Buy tables, because they are just branded copies of bog-standard cards. Hence, if you want to raise money for a particular charity or club, then you'd be better off using a Best Buy cashback card. You can then donate your annual rebate, plus an extra 28% on top from Gift Aid, to your favourite cause.

Annual fees

Although annual fees were fairly widespread in the Eighties and early Nineties, they largely died out by the mid-Nineties. Today, few credit cards charge an annual fee. Although it may make sense to pay an annual fee in return for additional benefits, it is difficult to place a value on these add-ons. Usually, these benefits cost more than they are worth.

As 99% of credit cards don't charge an annual fee, paying one is largely optional. Therefore, my advice would be to steer clear of credit cards which come with an annual fee attached.

Card protection plans

In return for a yearly fee of around £15 to £25, you can buy protection against fraud if your plastic cards are lost or stolen. With
one phone call, you can cancel and re-order all of your plastic
cards, plus you're covered against fraudulent transactions. The
two major providers of these plans are Card Protection Plan (CPP)
and Sentinel.

Although this protection may seem valuable, it is unnecessary
and overpriced. Indeed, if you are an honest victim of credit card
fraud or theft, then the law restricts your liability to just £50. In
many cases, credit card issuers will absorb all fraud costs for
honest customers. Therefore, as credit card issuers and plan
providers enjoy juicy profit margins on these card protection
plans, they are best avoided. Instead, take great care with your
plastic cards and don't let them out of your sight!

Cash withdrawals

Put simply, cash withdrawals and credit cards do not mix. In fact,
the golden rule of plastic cards is: *never use credit cards to withdraw
cash, as that's what debit cards are for!* If you do use a credit card
to withdraw cash from a cash machine or over the counter, then
you face four pitfalls:

1   You pay interest from the withdrawal date until your entire
    balance (including interest) is repaid in full. There is no
    interest-free period for cash withdrawals on credit cards.

2   Interest rates for cash withdrawals are hugely higher than
    those for purchases. So, expect to pay a rate of 20% to 30%
    APR for the privilege of withdrawing cash on your credit card.

3   You pay a cash withdrawal fee up to 3% of the amount
    withdrawn, with a minimum fee of, say, £3.

4   When you repay your bill, your repayments will reduce your
    cheapest debt first. This means that interest will continue to
    build up on expensive cash withdrawals until your balance
    is zero. This practice is known as a 'negative payment
    hierarchy' (see below).

Thus, taking out just £10 could cost you a small fortune in interest and fees. So don't do it except in extreme emergencies!

Cashback, loyalty and reward cards

With a cashback credit card, you can earn as you spend. However, these cards are only suitable for disciplined cardholders who always pay off their monthly bill in full. A typical cashback card pays an annual rebate of between 0.5% and 1% of your spending. This reward is usually made as a yearly credit to your account, or a cheque is sent to you.

When shopping around for a cashback card, choose your card with care. Some cards offer enhanced cashback for an introductory period, which makes them more valuable for short-term spending. Others pay higher rates of cashback on certain spending, such as petrol or supermarket shopping. So, do your homework by analysing your monthly spending before picking a cashback card.

Although cashback may appear to be easy money, don't be tempted into spending more than you can afford to repay on a cashback card. Also, you may forfeit your cashback if you don't pay on time, miss a repayment, or go over your credit limit. Hence, it makes sense to set up a direct debit to repay your entire monthly balance.

Chip and PIN

Chip and PIN (Personal Identification Number) was introduced in order to improve card security and reduce fraud. When using your credit card in person, you must enter a four-digit PIN in order to approve transactions. Never write down your PIN and never reveal it to another person. In addition, don't use the same PIN for several different cards. Otherwise, if your wallet or purse is stolen, then one PIN will unlock all of your accounts!

Credit balances

❝ credit cards are designed for spending, not saving ❞ Credit cards are designed for spending, not saving. Therefore, it makes no sense to build up a credit balance on a credit card, as this spare money will not earn any interest. Thus, if you do have a credit balance on a credit card, contact your card issuer to ask for a refund. A notable exception to this rule is the Egg Money credit card, which does pay interest on credit balances.

Credit card cheques

Credit card issuers send cheques to cardholders in order to encourage them to borrow more. The best of these cheques can be very useful as they offer extended interest-free credit on payment of a handling fee. For example, 10 months' interest-free credit for a 3% fee is a pretty good deal.

Then again, some credit card cheques can be very nasty. The worst kind are treated as cash withdrawals, so they charge sky-high rates of interest, have no interest-free period and come with hefty fees attached. So, check carefully before using a credit card cheque!

Credit limits are not targets

It's crucial to remember that credit should be used as sparingly as possible. Therefore, you should always regard your credit limit as a maximum ceiling and not a target. So, with a credit limit of £3000 and an outstanding balance of £1000, you do *not* have a spare £2000 to spend!

Direct debits and standing orders

If you don't pay on time, or miss a monthly repayment, then there may be serious consequences. First, you could pay a fine of around £12 for breaching the terms and conditions of your card. Second, you could lose any special-rate deals, such as a 0% balance transfer. Third, you could lose your standard interest-free period. Fourth, any missed repayments may be recorded on your credit record.

Therefore, it makes sense to automate your repayments so that you don't have to worry if you're forgetful or not good with paperwork. Setting up a monthly direct debit or standing order to take care of your repayments is a sensible move. Usually, your card issuer will allow you to pay your entire balance, a set amount, or your minimum monthly repayment. Ideally, you should pay as much as you can comfortably afford, as you can always make further payments if spare cash is available.

Extended warranties

A few credit cards offer a free extended warranty on electrical goods bought on plastic. Typically, this warranty applies to goods costing £50+ and extends the manufacturer's guarantee by a further year. In order to benefit from this warranty, you will need to register items with your credit card issuer. However, these warranties are not all-inclusive and should not be regarded as a substitute for a manufacturer's or retailer's guarantee.

Fraud

If your card is lost or stolen, or its details are used to purchase something without your permission, then you enjoy certain legal rights under the Consumer Credit Act. If you are not at fault, then your financial liability is capped at £50. However, if you have been careless with your card, or have revealed your PIN to another person then you could lose this protection. Therefore, you should treat your credit card and accompanying paperwork as carefully as if they were cash. Otherwise, you have a lot to lose ...

Free legal protection (Section 75)

Section 75 of the Consumer Credit Act provides you with valuable legal protection when you buy goods or services on a credit card. When you buy an item costing between £100 and £30,000 on a credit card (but not a debit card), you have a claim against your card issuer if something goes wrong. What's more, even if you've only paid a deposit of as little as £1 on your credit card, you can claim a refund of your entire financial loss.

Therefore, if an item is damaged, faulty or doesn't arrive, or the supplier goes bust, your card issuer must make good your loss. In layman's terms, it 'stands in the shoes of the supplier'. This protection also applies to purchases made overseas or from foreign websites. This extra protection explains why it makes sense to use a credit card (rather than a debit card) to pay for expensive purchases.

Gold and Platinum cards

Before credit cards became so widely used, Gold and Platinum cards used to enjoy a certain social status. Now that everyone and his dog has a credit card, these cards have tarnished and provide little in the way of snob value. Indeed, these 'precious metal' credit cards sometimes have minimum income requirements of as little as £8000, so they are well within the reach of most adults. Don't be fooled, as all that glisters is not gold!

Interest-free period (short or none)

The standard interest-free period provided to cardholders ranges from between 45 and 59 days. However, there are a few credit cards which offer no interest-free period to card users. These 'no credit' cards are designed for people who do not pay off their balance in full. These cards tend to be promoted on the basis of their below-average interest rate. However, better alternatives are available, such as 0% balance transfers and 0% on purchases cards.

Interest rates

Of course, interest rates vary widely from card to card. However, at the time of writing, the average interest rate charged on purchases was 16.5% APR. At this time, the Bank of England's base rate was just 5%. Therefore, a typical credit card charges an interest rate of more than three times the base rate.

What's more, credit card interest rates are largely unaffected by changes to the base rate and general interest rates. In short, regardless of what happens to the base rate, credit card interest rates remain uniformly high. Therefore, although credit cards may be appropriate for short-term borrowing, they become very expensive in the long run.

Late or missed repayments

Until mid-2006, credit card issuers imposed hefty fines on card-holders who failed to pay up on time. These penalties for late payments, missed payments and credit-limit breaches were as high as £25 per offence. However, following successful intervention by the Office of Fair Trading, the maximum penalty was reduced to £12.

Nevertheless, these penalty fees are still punitive, because they do not reflect the true cost of dealing with payment problems and credit breaches. In reality, these offences are managed by auto-mated, computerised processes and, therefore, cost no more than a few pounds to administer. In any event, it makes sense to keep an eye on your account in order to avoid these fines at all costs.

Lifetime balance transfers

One alternative to 0% balance transfers is the lifetime balance transfer. This charges a low interest rate until any transferred debts have been repaid in full. Typically, the interest rate on a lifetime transfer will be fairly close to the base rate – so, around 4% to 6% a year.

Thus, lifetime transfers allow you to borrow money over the long term without having to switch deals repeatedly. Then again, as with 0% transfers, most lifetime transfers attract upfront fees of 2% to 3%. These upfront fees make them more expensive in the short term, so do take these into account when weighing up the relative merits of lifetime transfers.

Minimum monthly repayments (MMRs)

Until the mid-Nineties, card firms would require cardholders to pay a minimum monthly repayment of at least a tenth (10%) of their outstanding debt. However, increased market competition and a surge in borrowing levels led card issuers to slash their MMRs. Once one card firm cut its MMR, the others followed suit. As a result, minimum monthly repayments tumbled from 10% to 5%. Later, they were trimmed to 3%, 2.5% and even as low as 2%.

Lower MMRs provide a huge benefit to card companies. The lower the repayment, the longer a debt takes to repay. Of course, this leads to bigger interest bills for borrowers and higher returns for lenders. Thus, the collapse in minimum repayments has enriched bankers at the expense of everyday borrowers.

Indeed, MMRs are now so slim that they mainly consist of interest and other charges. In other words, they barely reduce your debt at all. Incredibly, a debt of just £2500 can take over 25 years to repay, using a minimum monthly repayment of 2.5% (minimum £5)!

So, if you don't want a debt which drags on for decades, then avoid minimum monthly repayments. Instead, set up a direct debit or standing order for an affordable amount, say, a twentieth (5%) of your balance. By paying a fixed monthly sum (and throwing extra cash at your debt when you can afford it), you will pay off your balance in months or years, rather than decades.

Negative payment hierarchy

Almost all credit cards treat distinct types of debt in different ways. For example, cash withdrawals will always attract higher interest rates than purchases. In turn, purchases will almost always be more expensive than balance transfers.

When it comes to repaying card balances, almost all credit card issuers apply what's known as a 'negative payment hierarchy'. This technique allows them to allocate your monthly repayments towards your cheapest debt first. In other words, 0% balance transfers are repaid first, followed by purchases, with cash and cash-like transactions at the back of the queue.

As you'd expect, this system maximises the amount of interest paid by the cardholder. It's yet another example of lenders winning and borrowers losing. In mid-2008, of the major credit card issuers, Nationwide BS was the only firm to play fair by applying a positive payment hierarchy.

Networks: MasterCard, Visa and American Express

Almost all credit cards are affiliated to one of three major electronic payment networks. The largest of these networks is MasterCard, then Visa, with American Express (AMEX) bringing up the rear. While MasterCard and Visa process point-of-sale transactions, their member banks provide lending facilities to customers. Conversely, AMEX acts as both processor and lender. All three networks charge merchant fees to retailers for the use of their payment systems.

Payment protection insurance (PPI)

Credit card issuers love to make money from add-ons, particularly insurance policies. Perhaps the most profitable is payment protection insurance, or PPI. This optional insurance meets your monthly repayments if you are unable to work due to an accident, sickness or unemployment. In addition, it pays off any outstanding debt on your death.

However, payment protection insurance is incredibly overpriced – and this applies doubly for credit card repayment protection (CCRP). Indeed, this protection can be up to 10 times as expensive as its core cost, making it one of the UK's biggest financial rip-offs. You can learn more about this insurance in Chapter 5. For now, it's enough to know that PPI should be avoided like the proverbial plague!

Price and purchase protection

With certain credit cards, if you buy an item which is later reduced in price in a sale (or you find it cheaper elsewhere) then price protection allows you to claim back the difference within a specified time period. However, this cover is fairly limited, as it usually applies to goods costing £50+ and lasts, say, 60 days from the purchase date.

With purchase protection, if you buy an item on your card that is lost, accidentally damaged or stolen within a certain period, then you can reclaim some or all of the cost from your card issuer. This can provide useful extra cover for fragile or high-value goods that are not covered by your home contents insurance. Typically, items costing £50+ are covered for up to 60 days, subject to a limit of, say, £1000 per item and £5000 per year.

Price and purchase protection are particularly useful at Christmas, especially when goods are later reduced in the January sales. However, do check the small print before claiming, as a whole host of exclusions and get-out clauses may apply. Some card issuers provide price and purchase protection at no cost, but it's probably not worth paying extra for such limited protection.

Travel accident insurance

Some credit cards, especially Gold and Platinum cards, provide free travel accident insurance when you use one to pay for a flight, holiday and so on. This insurance pays lump-sum benefits if you are killed or seriously injured while travelling in transport paid for using your card. For instance, payouts are made following death, loss of one or more limbs, loss of sight in one or both eyes, or permanent disability.

This cover only applies while travelling on a journey, and usually excludes medical and baggage cover. Therefore, it should not be confused with a comprehensive travel insurance policy. If anything, this should be viewed as a poor man's version of personal accident insurance.

Using credit cards overseas

Be very wary when using plastic cards overseas or on foreign websites. When you use a credit card abroad, your card issuer will add a 'foreign currency commission' to the cost of each purchase. This 'loading fee' usually adds around 3% to the cost of each transaction. Thus, spending £1000 on your credit card during a holiday or business trip could cost you an extra £30.

We Brits spend around £12 billion a year overseas using plastic cards. Thus, this sneaky charge sets us back up to £360 million a year. In mid-2008, two card issuers which did not slap on this currency-conversion fee were Nationwide BS and the Post Office.

For more information on choosing and using credit cards, visit the following websites:

The Motley Fool: *www.fool.co.uk* (I write for this website)
Moneyfacts: *www.moneyfacts.co.uk*
MoneySupermarket: *www.moneysupermarket.com.*

Store cards: the devil's debt

In many ways, store cards are very similar to credit cards, but with one notable difference: the rip-offs are taken to extremes. Indeed, store cards could be described as 'the crack cocaine of credit', because they can do serious damage, yet are surprisingly easy to acquire!

❝ for crafty card sharps, store cards can be a winner ❞

Around 11 million adults have a store-card account, and many of these use their store cards to benefit from interest-free credit, loyalty and reward schemes, discounts, promotions and special offers. Thus, for crafty card sharps, store cards can be a winner. However, thanks to shockingly high interest rates and amazingly overpriced payment protection insurance, store cards can easily become the devil's debt.

For example, the May 2008 edition of *Moneyfacts* magazine listed 29 different store cards, from *Argos* to *Warehouse*. For payments other than by direct debit, 10 store cards charged rates under 20% APR. The remaining 19 cards charged APRs of between 23.9% and 30.9%.

Overall, the average interest rate charged by a store card is 24.6% APR. This is around eight percentage points higher than the rate for a typical credit card. Therefore, on average, store cards charge almost 50% more interest – half as much on top – than credit cards!

Accordingly, the rules of the game for store cards are the same as those for credit cards. You should pay off your bill in full every month in order to avoid paying any interest. Likewise, you should reject payment protection insurance, which can cost between 1% and 1.5% of your monthly balance, regardless of whether or not you pay it off in full.

In summary, if you are short of financial discipline then steer clear of store cards. In the wrong hands, they do far more harm than good. Lastly, if you're paying interest on a store card then it would be a wise move to transfer these debts to a 0% credit card. Why pay yearly interest of 30%+ when you can pay nothing at all?

Current accounts and overdrafts

After credit cards, current account overdrafts are the most widely used forms of credit in the UK. When you go overdrawn, you produce a negative balance in your current account. In other words, you owe your bank money, because your balance has fallen below zero.

Alas, millions of Brits find themselves with 'more month than money' and unintentionally slip into the red before payday. Of course, this isn't a big problem, so long as you have agreed an approved overdraft limit with your bank. However, if you slip overdrawn without permission, then expect to be hit by high rates of interest and extreme penalty charges.

It's usually a mistake to rely on an overdraft in order to keep your finances afloat. Although approved overdrafts are convenient and fairly inexpensive in the short term, unapproved overdrafts are horrendously expensive. Indeed, the cost of a modest overdraft varies enormously, depending on whether it is approved or unapproved, and the tariff of charges linked to it.

What's more, interest rates on unauthorised overdrafts are roughly twice those of approved overdrafts. In May 2008, a typical authorised overdraft charged an interest rate of roughly 12% a year. For unauthorised overdrafts, the yearly rate was close to 24% APR.

Furthermore, with a Best Buy current account, an approved overdraft can cost you nothing for a year, thanks to introductory 0% offers. At the other end of the scale, a short-lived unauthorised overdraft of just £50 could leave you out of pocket to the tune of, say, £150!

Unfair charges: the OFT versus the banks

In the first half of 2006, the Office of Fair Trading (OFT) announced that it considered credit card fines for late or missed repayments to be unfairly high. Thus, the OFT urged card issuers to reduce these default fees to no more than £12 per offence. This action proved to be highly successful, with default fees now ranging from £8 to £12.

After this victory, the OFT then turned its attention to unfair overdraft charges, relying on the 'fairness' elements of the Unfair Terms in Consumer Contracts Regulations. Unfortunately, the banks refused to play ball, forcing the OFT to bring legal action against eight leading providers of current accounts.

Some current account providers levy fines of up to £40 on customers who go overdrawn without permission, exceed their overdraft limit, or 'bounce' payments such as cheques, direct debits and standing orders. In 2007, banks paid out hundreds of millions of pounds to customers who sued in order to reclaim these unfair charges.

In order to stem a flood of similar cases, the banks and the OFT agreed to bring a test case in order to settle this issue once and for all. This test case began in early 2008, but the final outcome may not arrive until 2009 or 2010. In the meantime, all court cases and complaints to the Financial Ombudsman Service regarding unfair bank charges are on hold, pending the outcome of the OFT's court battle. However, you can still file a new claim, which will be on hold until the court case has ended.

Given that the true cost of handling unauthorised overdrafts is a few pounds per offence, it seems likely that the OFT will eventually win its battle against the banks. The hope is that the OFT wins through and imposes a cap on bank charges, similar to the £12 ceiling imposed on credit card issuers.

However, this victory could turn out to be a poisoned chalice. British banks make around £3.5 billion each year from unauthorised overdrafts. If this income were halved, banks would lose £1.75 billion a year. As a result, they would most likely raise charges elsewhere. For example, a yearly account fee of £50 charged to the UK's 40 million current accounts would raise £2 billion a year. So, once again, it's win some, lose some!

❝ it makes sense to keep a close eye on your bank's charges for unapproved overdrafts ❞

Therefore, it makes sense to keep a close eye on your bank's charges for unapproved overdrafts. Always try to avoid going overdrawn without permission. Instead, plan ahead by arranging an approved overdraft limit sufficient to meet your short-term borrowing needs. Also, watch out for any news on the ongoing court case ...

Avoiding extortionate overdraft penalties

In short, you should take great care to avoid going overdrawn without permission. If money is getting tight, call or e-mail your bank in order to ask for a temporary overdraft or an extension to your existing borrowing limit. Even if your bank charges a fee for this service, say, £20, this is likely to be far cheaper than running up an unauthorised overdraft.

Some banks do provide a safety net in the form of a small interest-free overdraft or a fee-free overdraft buffer. These prevent charges and interest being run up if you go just a few pounds into the red. Nevertheless, you should always pay close attention to your regular bills and large purchases. Otherwise, if you take your eye off the ball, a small unapproved overdraft can snowball into a big problem. Remember: going into the red can leave you with a sore head!

Finally, if you're unhappy with your bank's charges or service then vote with your feet. By shopping around for a Best Buy current account, you could save yourself hundreds of pounds a year in unnecessary charges. Thanks to an improved Banking Code, it's never been easier to switch accounts. Most switchers have managed to move within two weeks, with few reporting any major hitches, thanks to the help of dedicated switching teams at their new banks.

Unsecured personal loans

A personal loan is a bit like a mortgage, in that you borrow a fixed sum and repay it over a preset period. However, unlike a mortgage, an unsecured personal loan is not secured (you don't say!). Thus, unlike a mortgage, an unsecured loan does not 'take a charge' over your home, so it doesn't put your home at risk. Each year, around six million adults take out an unsecured loan, often to replace existing debts or pay for a car, holiday, home improvements, wedding or similar outlay.

The basic rules of borrowing also apply when it comes to personal loans. These 12 questions will help you to find your perfect personal loan.

1 *Do I need a loan at all?*
   As I have explained previously, it's best to avoid borrowing wherever possible (except for major purchases, to invest in your education, or to grow a business). In other words, avoid borrowing money simply to subsidise your lifestyle. Instead, aim to live below your means!

Rather than borrowing, why not try saving up for all but the biggest purchases? By doing this, you earn interest on your savings, instead of paying interest on a loan. In addition, the price of many big-ticket consumer goods tends to fall over time, so delaying your spending could mean bagging a bigger bargain.

2 *How much should I borrow?*

Never be tempted to borrow more than you need, as this will cost you more in the long run. For instance, if you need £7500 towards a new car, don't be tempted into borrowing £10,000 and putting the surplus towards a holiday or other spending. Over-borrowing will increase your interest bill and monthly repayments, ramping up your debt even further.

Of course, the shorter the period of your loan, the lower your interest bill will be. Therefore, it makes sense to repay your loan over as short a period as possible, while making sure that the higher monthly repayments are still affordable.

3 *Should I borrow against my home?*

These days, you can't throw a dart at a newspaper without hitting an advertisement for secured loans. Alas, the big problem with secured loans is that your home is at risk if you fail to keep up your repayments. During the housing crash of the early Nineties, tens of thousands of homeowners saw their properties seized by secured loan providers. Given the recent slide in house prices and lending levels, we may see a return to the 'bad old days' of high mortgage arrears and repossessions.

So, do think twice before borrowing against your home for non-essential purposes. Although it may make sense to get a secured loan or extend your mortgage in order to pay for home improvements, the same can't be said for a flashy new car or luxury holiday!

4 *What about a consolidation loan?*

One popular option for people with multiple debts is to roll up these debts into a single debt, known as a 'consolidation loan'. Often, these loans are advertised using phrases such as 'clear your debts', 'one easy monthly repayment' or 'lower monthly repayments'.

While consolidating existing debts into a new loan may seem like a good idea, it often backfires. Indeed, rolling up your debts and repaying them over a longer period can actually increase, rather than reduce, your total interest bill. What's more, a large proportion of people arranging consolidation loans go on to build up fresh debts to accompany their new loan. One survey put this figure as high as 83%, or five in every six 'consolidators'.

So, before arranging a consolidation loan, make sure that you recognise your underlying problem. In most cases, this will be a failure to budget which leads to spending more than you earn. Thus, cutting back on your spending is likely to be more successful than rolling up your debts and continuing to live the high life!

5 *Where should I look?*

There's little point in spending hours slogging from branch to branch in a fruitless attempt to compare what's on offer. The best place to look for loans is online, as you can compare hundreds of loans with a one-minute search on a price-comparison website. What's more, many Best Buy loans are only available via the Internet, making it a must-have resource for brighter borrowers.

6 *Are APRs reliable?*

The law requires all lenders to display a standardised annual percentage rate (APR) when advertising credit. However, this guide to interest rates is not terribly trustworthy. For example, adding rip-off payment protection insurance will bump up the cost, but will not alter an APR. Also, an upfront payment holiday will reduce an APR while increasing the overall interest bill. Also, thanks to 'individual pricing', the rate shown may be a 'typical' APR, for which you may not qualify.

The only reliable way to compare the true cost of personal loans is to check the total amount repayable (TAR). The TAR combines all charges for credit, including the advance, interest and application fees. So, your benchmark for comparing loans is the TAR, not the APR! If you don't see the TAR on your paperwork (it must be shown by law), then ask for this figure.

7 *Is the rate fixed or variable?*
Although the vast majority of personal loans charge a fixed interest rate throughout their life, some lenders do offer variable-rate loans. With a fixed-rate loan, your monthly repayments remain the same during the term of your loan. However, with a variable-rate loan, your monthly repayments could rise or fall over time, usually in line with general interest rates.

So, if you want the security of static monthly repayments then choose a fixed-rate loan. Alternatively, if you believe that you could benefit from lower rates in future then you may prefer a variable-rate loan. However, your choice of variable-rate loans will be very limited, so you may be better off by going down the fixed route.

8 *Am I a typical customer?*
Until the late Nineties, personal loans would charge the same rate of interest to all borrowers. Nowadays, lenders prefer to price their loans based on a borrower's personal circumstances, credit history and ability to repay. This 'risk-based pricing' now applies to more than eight in 10 personal loans.

In theory, two in three borrowers (67%) should be given the advertised 'typical APR'. However, crafty lenders have found ways to manipulate this guideline. They can do this by rejecting less appealing applicants and 'cherry picking' the best borrowers. For example, with 10 applicants, seven may be rejected outright, two receive the typical APR, and one is offered a higher rate. Thus, two-thirds of loans carry the typical APR, but only two in 10 applicants received it.

Therefore, if you don't have a spotless credit history (or have reason to believe that you would not qualify for the

❝ look for a lender which charges the same rate to all applicants ❞

headline rate), then look for a lender which charges the same rate to all applicants. You will find it hard to get first-rate credit if you have a history of missed credit repayments, have defaulted on previous debts, or have County Court judgments against you.

9   *Are the interest rates tiered?*
It's a general rule with personal loans that the more you borrow, the lower the interest rate. For example, a loan of £1000 might charge interest at 19.9% APR, whereas a large loan, say, £15,000 might come in at 7.9% APR.

It's worth noting that these interest-rate thresholds usually apply to round numbers, particularly £5000, £10,000 and £15,000. Thus, it may be more expensive to borrow, say, £4999 than it would be to borrow £5,001 (just £2 more). So, always check to see if the total amount repayable will fall if you step up into a lower interest-rate tier. Then again, don't be tempted to borrow a lot more than you need merely to bring down your interest rate. Generally speaking, this is a false economy!

10   *Should I buy PPI (payment protection insurance)?*
No, because payment protection insurance is a massive swindle. In June 2008, the Competition Commission unveiled its provisional findings into the market for loan PPI. It found that this market was anti-competitive, and that lenders' control of the distribution of loan PPI had pushed up prices and harmed consumer choice.

Therefore, my advice is simple: *never* buy PPI directly from a lender. Instead, if you must have this cover, then shop around for Best Buy independent, stand-alone PPI policies from the likes of www.BritishInsurance.com. (You can learn more about this overpriced protection, and other insurance rip-offs, in Chapter 5.)

11   *Are there any additional fees?*
When comparing the cost of personal loans, be sure to check whether any additional fees apply. For example, there may be upfront arrangement fees or an extra settlement fee

which accompanies your final repayments. Also, some lenders have resorted to charging steep fees for delivering your money to you quickly.

For example, a lender might charge £50 to deliver a cheque to you by courier, or up to £35 for a same-day bank transfer via CHAPS. Personally, I'd avoid these express delivery services and plump for a free bank transfer via BACS, which takes three to five working days.

12 *Are there any early-settlement penalties?*
While some lenders charge no penalty for early repayment of a loan, others will charge up to two months' extra interest. As around seven in 10 personal loans are repaid early, it makes sense to confirm any early-settlement charges before signing on the dotted line. Otherwise, you could be out of pocket if you decide to pay off your loan before it's due or replace it with a new loan.

Getting out of debt

For many people – those who are keen to get out of debt – this may well be the most important section of my book. However, I'm going to keep this section relatively short and simple. My aim is to give you some bait, rather than force-feeding you a banquet. I do this because, at the end of the day, only you can do the work that will dynamite your debts.

By now, having got this far through my book, you should be getting to grips with the basics of budgeting, spending and borrowing. Consequently, you should already possess most of the tools required to dig yourself out of debt. For example, you must understand the importance of spending less than you earn, minimising the amount of interest you pay, and maximising the amount of interest you earn.

Alas, with Britons the most indebted society on earth, problem borrowers are a growing breed. Indeed, in 2006/07, 1.7 million people with debt problems sought help from volunteers at the charity Citizens Advice. Nevertheless, when it comes to determining the scale of someone's debt problem, I divide borrowers into three separate groups:

Group one: stragglers

People who could easily take a knife to their debts, but have yet to do so, I call 'stragglers'. They may have missed a repayment or two, but have the capacity to pay off their debts without outside intervention. For most stragglers, getting out of debt involves directing their disposable income in a manner which pays off their existing debts as quickly as possible.

Group two: strugglers

One step down from stragglers are strugglers. These borrowers frequently struggle to make ends meet, and often rely on credit to subsidise their lifestyle. Paying off their existing debts over a reasonable period will be hard work, but it can be done with outside help from professional debt counselling services. Usually, this will involve freezing interest and reducing monthly repayments to an affordable level.

Group three: strangled

A further step down brings us to the most desperate of the debt-ridden: the strangled. For these people, their debt burden has become so heavy that it is squeezing the life out of their finances. In many cases, their non-mortgage debts dwarf their annual earnings, making it hugely unlikely that they will ever get back into the black. These unfortunate individuals must decide whether to make a fresh start by filing for insolvency or bankruptcy.

Are you are a straggler?

On the whole, stragglers have yet to fall into the deep pit marked debt. Indeed, along with a few debts, they may have some savings as well. Some stragglers are just financially disorganised; others may be getting a little too keen on living with debt.

Occasionally, a red flag goes up to warn stragglers that they aren't fully in control of their finances. For example, they may have 'more month than money' when last month's wage runs out before next month's wage arrives. They may incur the odd penalty fine for slipping overdrawn or for late or missing payments on a credit card.

It's important to note that stragglers still have their heads above water and are not yet out of their depth. Through better budgeting, they can put their debts on a diet and get their finances back on an even keel in what should be a relatively short space of time, say, within two years or so.

Help for stragglers

Of the three groups of borrowers, the stragglers are in the best position. In many cases, their problems are caused by simple financial mismanagement and can be solved relatively easily. For example, with a half-decent credit history, they can transfer interest-bearing debts to a 0% credit card, thus freezing their interest bill.

In most cases, stragglers will not need any outside help in order to tackle their debts. By maximising their disposable income through better budgeting and money management, they can release sufficient funds to pay off their debts in a relatively short space of time.

One of the best tools for stragglers is 'snowballing'. Snowballing is a simple concept: in short, it involves paying off your debts in order of the rates of interest which they attract. For example, take the table below:

Debt	Amount owed	Interest rate (APR)	Minimum monthly repayment
CostlyCard	£2,000	25%	£60
AverageCard	£1,500	15%	£45
BargainCard	£7,500	7%	£300
Total	£10,000	–	£405

As you can see, this borrower owes £10,000 and has minimum monthly repayments totalling £405. However, he can afford to pay £500 a month towards his debts. So, where should his surplus £95 a month go? Towards his largest debt, the £7500 on his BargainCard? Towards his smallest debt, the £1500 on his AverageCard? Actually, this extra cash will do the most good when it chips away at his most expensive debt, the £2000 on his CostlyCard which is costing 25% a year.'

So, the above borrower should make only minimum monthly repayments to his two cheaper cards. At the same time, he should pay £155 a month (£60 plus the spare £95) onto his CostlyCard. Once this debt has been extinguished, this spare £155 a month should be added to the £45 a month due on his AverageCard, boosting his monthly repayment to £200.

Likewise, once his AverageCard has been cleared, only his cheapest debt remains. By this time, the full £500 a month can be thrown at this debt, eliminating this final debt in record time. This method is known as snowballing because your snowball (the spare cash available to throw at your most expensive debt) gets bigger and bigger over time as previous debts die.

By the way, some stragglers may be tempted to roll up their existing debts into an unsecured personal loan. Before you do this, go back to my earlier comments on consolidation loans. For most people, snowballing delivers the goods better than 'clearing' debts using a loan.

Are you a struggler?

Strugglers are sinking deeper into the quicksand that is debt. As well as problems with budgeting, they struggle to pay both their basic bills and their monthly debt repayments. Usually, strugglers have little or nothing in the way of savings. Hence, large or unexpected outgoings, such as Christmas or a boiler breakdown, often or always end up being paid for on credit.

When things get really tight, strugglers may do something dangerous, like paying this month's mortgage payment using a credit card. Generally speaking, strugglers have much higher levels of debt than stragglers. Indeed, their outstanding balances may be so high that they have no choice but to pay merely the minimum monthly repayments demanded by their credit cards. For strugglers, life is all about running to stand still.

❝ for strugglers, life is all about running to stand still ❞

Help for strugglers

In my view, the extra challenges faced by strugglers mean that they need outside help to dig themselves out of debt. For example, their household budget and credit limits could be so stretched that they are unable to meet both their household expenses and their debt repayments.

One way out of this problem would be to convince lenders to freeze or suspend interest on your debts. Another might be to agree a write-off of some of your outstanding balances, in order to reduce your debt burden. However, lenders are naturally reluctant to agree to do this, because they are in the business of lending money for interest, plus they hate bad debts.

Of course, you could try negotiating with lenders yourself, but you won't have much leverage. You'll have far more success by getting a professional debt management firm to do the talking for you. At this point, I will direct you to one of these charities:

- The Consumer Credit Counselling Service (CCCS) at *www.cccs.co.uk* (0800 138 1111);

- National Debtline at *www.nationaldebtline.co.uk* (0808 808 4000);

- Citizens Advice at *www.adviceguide.org.uk* (telephone number in your local directory).

Be warned: almost all other debt management firms aim to profit from your misery. Indeed, a quarter (25%) of your monthly repayments could be pocketed by the company 'helping' you with your debts. So, stick to the three highly recommended charities shown above, and steer clear of debt vultures!

Are you strangled?

The strangled are in desperate straits, because debt has grown to dominate their life. As debt breeds yet more debt in a downward spiral, their household budget blows up, sometimes spectacularly. With outgoings larger than their earnings, the strangled are often forced to borrow from one lender to pay another.

What's more, they have problems with paying the key bills necessary for continued financial survival. The dangers increase when they miss payments or stop paying these bills: Council Tax and other personal taxes, mortgage or rent, Television Licence, energy bills, and so on. These payment problems normally lead to the involvement of debt collectors, bailiffs and other unwelcome visitors.

The most strapped of the strangled face impossible positions, such as being forced to choose between eating and heating. Eviction or house repossession can occur as a result of severe rent or mortgage arrears. In the end, overwhelming debt forces many of the most besieged borrowers to seek protection in the form of insolvency or bankruptcy.

Help for the strangled

For the strangled, only outside help will ensure financial survival so it's back to the three debt counsellors mentioned above. The worst-off of the strangled, such as those with debts several times their annual income, one possible outcome is to enter into personal insolvency or bankruptcy.

Insolvency: the Individual Voluntary Arrangement (IVA)

Personal insolvency takes the form of an Individual Voluntary Arrangement. These are the 'debt solutions' advertised heavily in the media. With an IVA, you come to an arrangement with lenders on how to repay your debts. This legal arrangement is administered by a licensed insolvency practitioner, usually a solicitor or accountant.

An IVA is legally binding and prevents further recovery action by your creditors. However, an IVA costs an average of £7500 to set up – money which is recouped from your monthly repayments. Typically, an IVA will run for up to five years. Your insolvency practitioner will keep an eye on your spending, can use some of your housing wealth to repay part of your debts, and use future pay rises to increase your monthly repayments.

It's important to note that insolvency is by no means an 'easy way out'. Indeed, if you fail to stick to the terms of your IVA then your insolvency practitioner must make you bankrupt. Speaking of which ...

Bankruptcy – the last resort

Bankruptcy is the final step in the slide towards debt disaster. Any creditor which is owed £750+ can apply to the court to make you bankrupt. However, in these debt-burdened days, it's more often the case that borrowers declare themselves bankrupt.

If you are made bankrupt then you stand to lose most of your assets, including your family home (although your pension may survive intact). Your financial affairs will be taken over by an official receiver or insolvency practitioner. This person will take over your assets and sell whatever s/he can in order to repay your creditors. During bankruptcy, any excess income you come by must be given to your handler. Furthermore, when dealing with banks, building societies and so on, you are obliged to confirm that you are a bankrupt.

The only good news is that honest bankrupts are automatically discharged after one year. However, you remain liable for your debts for a further three years. After this, your remaining debts (other than Student Loan Company debts) will be written off, leaving you as a 'discharged' bankrupt.

Then again, you should not regard bankruptcy as a 'soft option'. During and after your bankruptcy, you face close scrutiny from the official receiver. Any attempt to wriggle off the hook by avoiding your responsibilities can lead to severe penalties. What's more, bankruptcy effectively 'blows up' your credit record, leaving you unlikely to gain credit for at least six years.

On the other hand, reckless or dishonest bankrupts face tighter restrictions. Outright rogues could remain under supervision for up to 15 years, during which time they may be prevented from being a company director, obtaining credit of £500+, or trading under names other than their own. Breaching a 'Bankruptcy Restriction Order' of this type is a criminal offence.

Finally, bankruptcy procedures apply only in England, Wales and Northern Ireland. In Scotland, bankruptcy is known as Sequestration and the equivalent to an IVA is a Trust Deed.

The worst-case scenario: death by debt

This is such a controversial subject that I had to think carefully before including this footnote. All the same, I believe that the topic of 'suicide by debt' needs to be raised. Indeed, in recent years, there has been extensive press coverage of cases where borrowers have taken their lives in order to try to bring their debt problems to an end. Therefore, I feel obliged to say the following:

You owe lenders only money, not your life!

If debt has come to dominate your life, to the extent that you are depressed, anxious or are having trouble sleeping, then you *must* seek professional help without delay. Begin by visiting your GP to tackle your physical and mental health problems. At the same time, seek financial help from the likes of CCCS and National Debtline. If you really are at your wits' end, then call the Samaritans on 08457 909090 or visit *www.samaritans.org.uk*.

Finally, for a touching account from a GP of what happens to the people who are left behind by suicide victims, read this post on the popular Motley Fool website: *www.boards.fool.co.uk/Message. asp?mid=6616381.*

Taking care of your credit report

One way to keep tabs on your borrowing (and your future ability to borrow) is to keep an eye on your credit record, also known as your credit report, credit history, credit reference or credit file.

Information about your current and past credit history is kept by three credit reference agencies (CRAs). In order of size, the CRAs are Experian, Equifax and Callcredit. These businesses record vast amounts of information on how we Brits manage our personal financial affairs. These credit files are accessed by lenders and other organisations in order to establish our 'creditworthiness'.

Therefore, any negative or incorrect information in your credit record could prevent you from obtaining credit. Thus, it makes sense to check your credit record on occasion in order to make sure that it is accurate and up to date. Furthermore, monitoring your credit record enables you to spot abnormal transactions and could help to prevent you being a victim of fraud. If you do find any mistakes in your credit record, send a 'notice of correction' to the agencies, insisting that they update your files accordingly.

Although you can obtain a posted copy of your credit record for £2, online access to your files is considerably more expensive. However, the credit reference agencies frequently offer free trials of this online service. Typically, these 'try before you buy' offers last 30 days and allow you to examine your credit record for discrepancies, before cancelling at no cost. The most popular of these services is CreditExpert from Experian, which can be found at *www.creditexpert.co.uk.*

What's more, many lenders now use individual risk-based pricing in order to determine the interest rate paid by an applicant. Hence, making sure that your credit report is accurate could produce a better credit rating and give you access to lower loan rates, etc.

Keeping a clean credit record is largely down to common sense. Essentially, it boils down to paying your bills on time, meeting the monthly repayments on your credit agreements, and making sure that you do not exceed your credit limits. On the other hand, late and missed payments, other defaults, and court judgments will leave negative footprints on your credit record.

So, if you want to get credit in the future, then look after your debts today. Otherwise, the information on your credit record – both positive and negative – will stay on file for six years. Thus, any payment problems on credit cards, loans, mortgages and so on will linger for the next 72 months.

What's more, applying for credit too often can count against you when being credit-checked by lenders. This is because every application for credit – whether successful or otherwise – leaves a 'footprint' on your file. One of the downsides of being a '0% rate tart' is it marks you out as a skilled credit card player, which can make it hard to succeed when making future applications for credit. Then again, applying for credit once or twice a year is unlikely to do much harm, so stick to the 'must have' deals and avoid casually applying for more credit.

❝ one of the downsides of being a '0% rate tart' is it marks you out as a skilled credit card player ❞

In summary, your credit record should accurately reflect your current financial circumstances. If it doesn't, then it's up to you to correct any errors in order to keep a high financial standing. To do this, ask the relevant credit reference agency to amend any mistakes. If you wish to bring any additional information to the attention of lenders, then you can add a short note (around 200 words) to your credit file, known as a 'notice of correction'.

Websites for credit reference agencies

Experian   *www.experian.co.uk*

Equifax   *www.equifax.com*

Callcredit *www.callcredit.co.uk*

One final comment on credit

It's important to remember that British banks, building societies and other lenders make many billions every year from lending to individuals. Indeed, my guess is that our total personal debt of £1448 billion costs us close to £100 billion a year in interest alone!

So, be very wary when lenders queue up to throw handfuls of money in your direction. You may be creditworthy today, but who knows what may happen tomorrow? Always remember that by borrowing heavily to live for today, you are short-changing yourself tomorrow. In effect, you're stealing from your own future.

Lastly, when dealing with lenders, it pays to be a sceptic and a cynic. Indeed, always remember that it's not credit that lenders are offering, but debt. You have to admit, a *debt card* sounds much less attractive than a *credit card*, doesn't it?

chapter

3

How to be a happier homeowner

In the previous chapter, we looked at how to hang onto more of your money by borrowing as little as you can. Nevertheless, no matter how hard you save, it's highly likely that buying a home will plunge you into debt for many years to come.

Here in the UK, credit cards, overdrafts and personal loans are viewed as 'nasty debt'. On the other hand, a mortgage or home loan is seen as 'nice debt', because it enables you to buy the roof over your head. However, this distinction doesn't really make much sense, as debt that is 'good' for one person may prove to be 'bad' for another.

All the same, there is a crucial difference between home loans and other debts: mortgages are 'secured' on property or other assets, whereas unsecured debts (alias consumer credit) are not.

Secured lending

Secured lending does what it says on the tin. A loan is secured against one or more of your assets, usually your home or business. If you are unable to keep up repayments on a secured loan, then the lender can take action to seize the underlying asset and sell it in order to pay off what you owe. As secured lending is less risky for lenders than unsecured lending, interest rates on secured loans are usually much lower.

Many of us are familiar with the most common form of secured lending: a mortgage or home loan. Indeed, there are around 11.8 million mortgages in the UK, with total mortgage debt close to £1217 billion in July 2008. As well as homeowner mortgages, there are also further advances in the form of secured personal loans, second mortgages and charging orders. (Later in this chapter, I explain how a charging order can turn unsecured borrowing into a secured loan against your home.)

Let's look at mortgages in more detail.

How mortgages work

Few people know that the word 'mortgage' comes from the French words for 'dead' (*mort*) and 'promise' (*gage*). This makes home loans seem much more frightening than they really are. A promise until dead? They don't tell you this in your local bank branch!

Around a quarter (25%) of all homes are bought for cash. The remaining 75% are acquired using a mortgage. Although mortgages may appear complicated at first, in fact, they are remarkably simple beasts. A mortgage is simply a large loan which is secured against the property that it helps to purchase.

Generally speaking, a mortgage runs for 25 years, which means that the borrower must find 300 monthly repayments. The period or life of your mortgage is generally known as the term. Mortgage borrowers, like schoolchildren, keenly await the end of term and the ensuing holiday!

At this point, it's worth mentioning the wealth warning which accompanies all mortgage documentation:

Your home is at risk if you do not keep up repayments on a mortgage or other loan secured on it.

So, unlike other forms of borrowing, you could lose the roof over your head if you fall behind with your mortgage repayments. Indeed, if your lender feels that it has no other option, then it will repossess (seize) your home and sell it at auction. If the sale of your home does not realise enough money to pay off your debt including arrears, then the lender will pursue you for any outstanding amounts.

Happily, mortgage repossessions have tumbled since reaching a peak of 75,500 in 1991. Even though the housing market started to weaken in the second half of 2007, repossessions in 2008 may be around half of this peak figure. Another problem for homeowners is the threat of 'negative equity', when a property is worth less than the mortgage secured on it. We discuss this difficulty later in this chapter.

Four important questions to ask

In order to keep on top of your mortgage and remain a happy homeowner, you need to answer these four vital questions:

1 How much can I borrow?
2 How much can I really afford?
3 How do I want to repay my debt?
4 How do I want interest to be charged?

How much can I borrow?

Question one will be answered by your mortgage lender. In order to manage their risk, all mortgage lenders place limits on the absolute amounts of money that they are willing to lend to individual borrowers. Before the housing boom started to peak, most lenders would lend a single applicant up to four times his/her gross income (before deductions for tax, National Insurance and so on). For joint borrowers, lenders would draw the line at 2½ times their combined salaries.

As the housing bubble reached its peak in 2007, lenders rushed to lend homebuyers as much as they possibly could. At this time, it was possible for single applicants to borrow five, six or even seven times their gross income. However, the ensuing chaos caused by the worldwide credit crunch forced lenders to return to traditional measures of risk.

Thus, lenders have become much more cautious and have tightened up their lending criteria in order to minimise their exposure to high-risk borrowers. Nowadays, getting a mortgage of five or more times salary is only an option for graduate professionals such as young doctors and lawyers.

As computerised risk management has become increasingly more sophisticated, some lenders have resorted to using other methods to analyse affordability. For example, instead of relying on income multiples, they look at the affordability of mortgage repayments in the context of an applicant's household budget. In other words, they look at the borrower's take-home pay and outgoings in order to establish whether monthly repayments will be affordable.

❝ prudent buyers may be able to arrange a larger mortgage than the majority of homeowners ❞

In some circumstances, this method enables borrowers to obtain higher loans than they would using traditional methods. For example, borrowers with low or no other debts and modest outgoings will be in a good position to afford higher monthly repayments than the typical man in the street. Hence, these prudent buyers may be able to arrange a larger mortgage than the majority of homeowners.

How much can I really afford?

This is a question that only you can answer. Some people are naturally more adventurous than others, so they are willing to take on higher levels of personal debt. However, when it comes to your mortgage, it pays to be prudent. As a general rule of thumb, your mortgage repayments should account for no more than a third of your take-home pay.

The red warning light starts flashing when mortgage repayments exceed half of your household budget. At this level, you have very little room for manoeuvre and a sudden or steady increase in interest rates could leave you strapped for cash. One way to plan ahead sensibly is to budget for a 2% rise in your mortgage interest rate. By doing this, you ensure that you won't be caught short when your mortgage repayments climb upwards.

Of course, home ownership merely begins with mortgage repayments. On top of these, there is a whole host of one-off and ongoing costs to consider. You need to budget for repaying your loan at some point in the future (unless you have a repayment mortgage which chips away at your debt as you go along), stamp duty, valuation or survey fees, legal or conveyancing costs, household insurances, council tax, plus any fees and other charges relating to your home loan.

Thus, someone with champagne tastes and a beer income may find it difficult to pay out even a quarter of their income on mortgage repayments. On the other hand, someone with little or no debts and a good grasp of budgeting may be able to pay half of their income on mortgage repayments and still make ends meet. It really is down to you as to whether you make a success of buying a home!

How do I want to repay my debt?

Of course, a mortgage is a debt like any other, so you must make arrangements to pay it off at some point in the future. There are two basic ways to do this:

1   Using an *interest-only* mortgage. With an interest-only mortgage, your monthly repayments to your lender only meet the interest bill on your debt. Thus, your debt does not decrease over time and, when your mortgage expires, you must pay off this outstanding debt. If you are unable to do so, then you may be forced to sell your house and move to a smaller property. Ideally, borrowers with interest-only mortgages set up an investment plan which, over the years, increases in value until it is sufficiently large to redeem the mortgage.

2   Using a *repayment* mortgage. With a repayment mortgage, your monthly repayments are made up of both interest and capital repayments. In other words, you repay a little of your debt as you go and, over the life of your mortgage, you are

guaranteed to pay off the entire sum due. In the early years of your mortgage, your repayments will consist largely of interest and a tiny amount of capital. However, in the later years, repayments consist largely of capital repayments.

By the way, the housing boom which began in the mid-Nineties encouraged mortgage lenders to become much more creative with their product ranges. These days, it's possible to take out a mortgage over 30 or 40 years. By taking out a repayment mortgage over more than 25 years, you reduce your monthly repayments, but increase your total interest bill. This option should only be pursued by prospective homeowners desperate to jump onto the property ladder.

How do I want interest to be charged?

As with all loans, one crucial respect of a mortgage is the interest rate which you pay. In order fully to understand your mortgage, you should know the interest rate that you are paying and whether this will change over time. Let's look at your options when it comes to choosing how interest is charged.

Fixed-rate mortgages

With a fixed-rate mortgage, your interest rate and monthly repayments are fixed for a specific period. Therefore, during this time, you have the security of knowing exactly how much your mortgage will cost. Although most homeowners choose to fix their mortgage rate over two or three years, fixed rates are available for five, 10 or even 25 years.

Regardless of what happens to interest rates generally, the amount you pay will not change. Of course, when your fixed-rate deal expires, it's time to look around for another attractive interest rate. Nevertheless, it's worth noting that the arrangement fees associated with fixed-rate mortgages have increased dramatically in recent years.

For the record, fixed-rate mortgages only appeared in the UK in 1989, but quickly became increasingly popular. A few years ago, fixed-rate mortgages rarely came with an arrangement fee exceeding £500. These days, arrangement fees can exceed £2000 and can even amount to 3% of your loan. Thus, it is vital to look beyond the headline-grabbing interest rate and always take into account the fees associated with fixing your rate.

Capped rates

The first capped-rate mortgage was launched in the UK in 1990. With a capped rate, your interest rate is variable, but will not rise above a ceiling rate known as a 'cap'. In other words, the cap sets an upper limit on how high your mortgage interest rate can go. For example, with a capped rate of 6% a year, your mortgage rate will never exceed 6%. However, your interest rate will vary over time, as it will normally be linked to your lender's standard variable rate or to the Bank of England base rate.

Discounted rates

With a discounted rate, the interest rate you pay is linked to your lender's standard variable rate (SVR). However, you receive a discount on this SVR, so the rate you pay is always at a predetermined level below your lender's prevailing SVR. For example, with a 2% discount off an SVR of 7%, you will pay 5% a year.

Standard variable rate (SVR)

The standard variable rate is the rate that a lender charges all borrowers who are not on a special-rate deal. In short, it is the bog-standard interest rate which acts as a benchmark between lenders. Typically, the SVR is the highest rate charged by a lender, so it makes sense to avoid paying your lender's SVR wherever possible.

Tracker rates

A tracker rate does what it says on the tin: it tracks the Bank of England base rate. For example, with a 'base rate plus 0.5%' loan, the rate you pay will be half a percentage point above the base rate. Thus, if the base rate is 5% a year, then you will pay 5.5% with a base rate + 0.5% tracker loan.

Flexible mortgages

Flexible mortgages are sometimes called 'Australian' mortgages, because they were imported from Down Under in the early Nineties. With a flexible mortgage, your interest bill is calculated daily. Thus, any repayments you make immediately reduce your outstanding loan.

With traditional mortgages, known as 'annual rest' loans, your repayments would be held back until the end of the year, when they would be knocked off your loan all in one go. Thus, with a daily interest mortgage, you pay less interest over the life of your loan, all other things being equal.

The other benefit of a flexible mortgage is the ability to overpay in the good times, using lump sums, one-off or monthly amounts. Equally, when money is tight, you can underpay or take repayment holidays, usually without penalty. In addition, you won't be penalised for repaying your loan early. In fact, with a flexible mortgage, you're positively encouraged to pay down your loan faster.

It's worth noting that many modern mortgages include some repayment flexibility, so there's no need to pay a premium for a fully flexible loan.

Offset mortgages

An offset mortgage has many of the features of a flexible mortgage, but with one significant improvement. You can 'offset' your savings against your outstanding home loan in order to reduce your overall interest bill. Although your mortgage and savings are usually kept in different pots, you pay interest only on the difference between them. For instance, with a loan of £100,000 and offset savings of £20,000, you pay interest on your 'net debt' of £80,000.

For homeowners with considerable savings, combining these savings with an offset mortgage can be a very attractive prop-

"the interest you earn is 'tax free', which further boosts your returns "

osition. In effect, your savings earn interest at your prevailing mortgage rate. As mortgage rates are generally higher than savings rates, this can boost the return on savings. What's more, the interest you earn is 'tax free', which further boosts your returns.

Generally speaking, unless you have substantial savings worth, say, a fifth (20%) of your mortgage, then there's not much of an advantage to be had with an offset mortgage. If your savings are below this level, then the amount you gain from offsetting is largely cancelled out by the higher interest rates charged by these home loans.

Current account mortgages

The current account mortgage, or CAM, takes the offset mortgage one step further. By combining current account, savings and home loan, a CAM uses any spare cash in your current account to reduce your debt still further. Naturally, this credit balance further reduces your overall interest bill.

Here's an example:

- mortgage of £100,000
- less savings of £20,000
- less credit account balance of £2500
- gives a 'net debt' of £77,500, on which interest is charged.

Again, CAMs work best for disciplined borrowers who have substantial savings and keep their current account in credit. Conversely, if you misuse a CAM by constantly withdrawing your housing equity, then this could ultimately lead to you losing your home.

Now that we've covered the various types of mortgages, let's improve our knowledge yet further.

A–Z of home ownership

Annual Percentage Rate (APR)

In theory, an APR is meant to give you an indication of the cost of borrowing. However, in practice, it's not much use when shopping around and comparing mortgages. Indeed, mortgage APRs are complicated, difficult to calculate and open to manipulation. Therefore, when choosing a mortgage, don't use the APR as a benchmark. Instead, dig down into the small print and establish exactly how much you have to pay, including monthly repayments and all fees linked to your loan.

Application, booking, product and reservation fees

When choosing a mortgage, be sure to check for any upfront application, booking or reservation fees. These days, most special-rate mortgages (and even some SVRs) come with some form of upfront fee. You can pay this fee separately or add it onto your mortgage, which costs more in the long run.

Until a few years ago, the majority of mortgages came without any application fee. These days, it's rare to find a mortgage with no application fees whatsoever, and most special-rate deals charge fees ranging from £500 to £5000. Indeed, some lenders have taken to charging percentage-based fees, which can add a fee of 1% to 3% to a loan.

Generally speaking, percentage-based fees are less attractive for larger loans. For example, a 2.5% fee on a £400,000 loan means coughing up £10,000 or adding this sum to your mortgage.

Brokers

A mortgage broker is an intermediary who searches the market in order to find you an attractive mortgage deal. Then again, some brokers have links only to a limited number of lenders. As these brokers are unable to scour the entire market, they are best avoided. Instead, look for a whole-of-market broker who is able to cast his net as wide as possible.

Some brokers charge hefty fees for providing this service and advice. However, there are several no-fee brokers who will do the same job at no expense to you. These brokers rely on the procuration fees paid by lenders in order to make a living. Perhaps the most popular no-fee broker is London & Country Mortgages, whose website is at *www.lcplc.co.uk*.

Cashback mortgages

With a cashback mortgage, you receive a payment or 'gift' once your loan has been 'drawn down' (when your loan begins, usually on the completion date of your purchase). This cashback will be a percentage of your loan, usually between 3% and 8% of the amount borrowed. Of course, this isn't a free lunch: in return for the cashback, you agree to be locked into a particular mortgage rate for up to 10 years.

In most cases, cashback mortgages are linked to a lender's SVR, which is usually far from being a Best Buy. Therefore, I'm not a big fan of cashback mortgages, largely because of their inflexibility and the high rates they charge.

Conveyancing and legal fees

When buying or selling a property, you need the services of a solicitor or licensed conveyancer. Your legal fees will depend on the value of the property in question, and the amount of legal legwork involved. In the main, the legal costs incurred in buying or selling a house will usually fall between £500 and £2500. Hence, your budget should make suitable allowance for this additional cost.

Deeds release, exit, sealing and discharge fees

When you decide to pay off your home loan, your mortgage lender eagerly looks forward to slapping on yet more charges. In the early Nineties, these mortgage exit arrangement fees (MEAFs) amounted to £50 to £150. However, since the turn of the century, MEAFs have soared, with some lenders charging hundreds of pounds when discharging mortgages.

The Financial Services Authority (FSA) was unhappy with this trend, so it ordered mortgage lenders to treat their customers fairly. As a result, thousands of borrowers were able to reclaim inflated exit fees. Nevertheless, lenders continue to look for ways to boost their profit margins, so always ask about any fees which apply when you pay off or transfer your mortgage.

Deposit

If you want access to mortgage lenders' best deals, then you'll need to save up a deposit to put down on your home. Without a deposit, you will need to borrow the entire purchase price of a property, via a 100% mortgage, but these are few and far between these days. A 5% deposit (and a 95% mortgage) will give you access to slightly better mortgage interest rates. However, to access the lowest interest rates offered by lenders, you will need to find a deposit of 10% to 25% of the value of your home.

In the property boom of 1996 to 2007, no-deposit mortgages became widely available. Indeed, some lenders were happy to lend in excess of a property's value. At the peak of the mortgage frenzy, it was possible to borrow 125% or even 130% of the purchase price. In effect, these were 'negative equity' mortgages, since prices would have to rise substantially before homebuyers would own even a single brick.

❝ the larger your deposit, the lower your risk as a borrower ❞

The simple rule is: the larger your deposit, the lower your risk as a borrower, and the more attractive you become to mortgage lenders. So, if you want to buy a house in the next few years, then begin by saving hard!

Early repayment charge (ERC; also known as a 'redemption penalty')

An early repayment charge will apply if you decide to pay off your mortgage early. If you signed up to a very attractive special-rate deal, then this penalty could amount to thousands of pounds. So, before choosing a home loan or ditching an existing mortgage, do check to see whether a hefty redemption penalty applies.

Endowment mortgage

Endowment mortgages were very popular in the Eighties and early Nineties, but fell out of favour towards the end of the century. With an endowment mortgage, you have an interest-only home loan, plus an insurance policy. This policy does two things: first, it provides life insurance to repay your debt if you die. Second, your premiums also build up an investment pot, which may or may not grow sufficiently large to repay your loan at the end of its life.

The stock market crash which began in 2000 sounded the death knell for endowment mortgages. It revealed a toxic combination of high charges, poor investment returns and eye-popping commissions paid to salesmen. These days, new endowment mortgages are few and far between, so they can be safely ignored.

First-time buyers (FTBs)

First-time buyers are the foundation of the property market, because they underpin the first rung of the property ladder. However, since the mid-2000s, first-time buyers have struggled with housing affordability. As property prices rocketed upwards, FTBs became an increasingly rare breed. By 2008, the number of first-time buyers was hitting all-time lows. Alas, first-time buyers are unlikely to return to the market in droves until house prices have undergone a significant correction and home loans again become more freely available.

Higher lending charge (HLC; also known as a mortgage indemnity premium, or MIP)

Mortgage lenders don't like to be too heavily exposed to the risk of a property crash. Therefore, they prefer not to lend borrowers more than three-quarters (75%) of a property's purchase price. If you wish to borrow more than this 75% threshold, some lenders will charge you an additional fee. This is known as a higher lending charge.

In some cases, the HLC kicks in not at 75%, but at 90%. Indeed, some lenders levy no higher lending charge to borrowers who can stump up a 5% deposit. Nevertheless, a higher lending charge could add thousands of pounds to the cost of your loan. The HLC will vary depending on what percentage of the purchase price your mortgage comes to, and the premium rate charged by the lender.

Some lenders avoid higher lending charges by levying higher interest rates on borrowers with smaller deposits. So, to avoid HLCs altogether, try to put down as large a deposit as you can muster. And, again, be sure to ask about higher lending charges before signing on the dotted line.

House prices

If you buy a home when house prices are relatively high, then you will spend a greater proportion of your lifetime income on accommodation. Conversely, if you buy when house prices are relatively low, then your lifetime housing costs will be reduced (all other things being equal).

That said, it is incredibly difficult to decide when house prices are peaking and are due for a fall. However, take a look at the following figures for the average house price between 1996 and 2007 (using the Halifax House Price Index):

1996:	£66,094
2007:	£196,792
Increase:	198%

Thus, in the 12 years up to the end of 1997, house prices across the UK almost tripled. However, over the same period, average wages increased by a mere 63%.

Given that house prices have massively outpaced wage increases during this housing boom, it seems incredibly unlikely that house prices will continue their upward march. Indeed, house prices began to fall in late 2007 and this about-turn has continued into 2008. As the housing market weakens, it seems likely that it will take several years of falls before prices begin to rise again. But, without a crystal ball, who can say?

Insurance policies

Buying a home can be a risky business. Unexpected events can disrupt your finances and, in extreme circumstances, can lead to the loss of your home. In order to manage these risks, mortgage lenders are very keen to sell you various insurance policies. In general, insurance policies bought from mortgage lenders are expensive and provide fat profit margins to the lender.

So, watch out when your lender urges you to buy any of the following policies:

- critical illness insurance (to protect against serious illnesses);
- income protection (cover against long-term sickness);
- life insurance (to pay off your debt if you die);
- home insurance (building and contents cover); and
- mortgage payment protection insurance (MPPI; accident, sickness and unemployment cover)

As we learn in Chapter 5, you can save a fortune by shopping around for these and similar policies. If you don't want to be ripped off by your lender, then consult a reputable insurance broker or get online.

Interest rate

When weighing up mortgages, it's essential to look beyond the attractive interest rates which lenders advertise heavily. Whilst it's true that mortgage interest will account for the bulk of your home-buying costs, you should always take into account other one-off and ongoing costs. Otherwise, instead of considering the big picture, you end up looking at only a few pieces of the mortgage jigsaw.

The following table shows how higher interest rates can dramatically increase the amount you repay over the life of your mortgage.

Mortgage repayments per £100,000 borrowed (over 25 years)

Interest rate	Monthly repayments Interest-only	Repayment	Total repaid Interest-only	Repayment
4%	£333.33	£527.84	£100,000	£158,352
6%	£500.00	£644.30	£150,000	£193,290
8%	£666.67	£771.82	£200,000	£231,546
10%	£833.33	£908.70	£250,000	£272,610
12%	£1000.00	£1053.22	£300,000	£315,966
14%	£1166.67	£1203.76	£350,000	£361,128

As you can see, the monthly repayments for interest-only mortgages are always lower than those for repayment loans. Of course, this is because repayment mortgages chip away at the debt as you go along. Thus, at the end of the term, the mortgage is guaranteed to be paid off. Also, note that the figures in column four (showing the total repaid under an interest-only mortgage) do not include the lump sum required to pay off the loan at the end of the term (£100,000 in the above example).

Obviously, as interest rates rise, so too do your monthly repayments. For example, with an interest-only mortgage, a tripling of interest rates from 4% to 12% would also triple your repayments. However, this effect is reduced for repayment mortgages: in the same scenario, your repayments would only double. Thus, thanks to their element of capital repayment, monthly repayments for repayment mortgages are less volatile than those for interest-only mortgages.

Lodgers

One way to boost your home-buying budget is to share your housing costs by taking in a lodger. Under the government's 'Rent a Room' scheme, you can earn up to £4250 a year, tax free, by allowing someone live under your roof. However, any rent in excess of this yearly limit will be taxed as unearned income.

Longer loans

Traditionally, home-buyer mortgages are arranged over 25 years, which means handing over 300 monthly repayments. However, as houses have become more expensive, mortgage lenders have come up with new ways to make home-buying more affordable. One trick is to allow borrowers to spread their repayments over a longer period.

Thus, it's now possible to take out a mortgage over 30 or even 40 years. The problem with going down this route is that the longer the loan, the higher the total interest bill. Therefore, by increasing the length of your loan by five or 10 years, you can bring down your monthly repayments by a few pounds. However, doing this will lead to the total interest paid rising by thousands of pounds. So, think twice before signing up to a 'lifetime loan'!

❝ think twice before signing up to a 'lifetime loan'! ❞

Negative equity

If you have a mortgage of £80,000 on a house worth £100,000, then your equity (the difference between a property's value and the mortgage secured on it) is £20,000. In this situation, your equity amounts to a fifth (20%) of the property's value.

However, if the property then falls in value to £80,000 and your mortgage remains the same, then your equity has been wiped out. Even worse, if the property dives again to just £70,000, then your mortgage is £10,000 more than the value of your home. In effect, you have 'negative equity' of £10,000.

Negative equity becomes a big problem when you decide to move home, remortgage or pay off your home loan. For example, during the housing crash of the early Nineties, negative equity caused many homeowners to hand back their house keys and walk away from their home loan. Although negative equity has all but vanished during the latest housing boom, it could rear its ugly head again if house prices continue to fall from their 2007 peak.

Re-mortgage

Of course, you're not tied to a single loan or lender during the life of your mortgage (unless you've signed up to a 25-year, fixed-rate mortgage, that is). Indeed, as one special-rate deal comes to an end, you should be looking around for an equally attractive replacement, say, three months beforehand. Replacing an existing home loan with a new mortgage is known as 're-mortgaging'.

You don't have to re-mortgage with the same lender, although this is often the cheapest option, as it avoids paying survey/valuation, legal and other fees. However, it always pays to shop around to locate the best deals available at the time. So, before your existing offer comes to an end, approach a no-fee, whole-of-market mortgage broker to see what's out there. Also, you are under no obligation to re-mortgage for exactly the same amount. You can take out a smaller loan, or 'unlock' capital from your home by opting for a larger mortgage.

Removals

Unless you plan to hire a van and conduct your house move yourself, then expect to pay between £500 and £1000 for the services of a professional removals firm. Be sure to get several quotes from reputable firms, ask around for recommendations, and check the website of trade association the British Association of Removers at *www.bar.co.uk*.

Repossession

Repossession is the word used by mortgage lenders to describe the seizure of properties from borrowers who are unable to keep up their repayments. Usually, repossessed properties are sold at auction and, if this sale does not realise enough to pay off any outstanding home loans, then lenders will chase borrowers for the remainder.

Second mortgages and secured loans

One cheap way to raise funds is to borrow against the value of your home. As mortgages are relatively low risk, the interest they charge is usually much lower than for other forms of borrowing. You can borrow against your home by increasing your existing mortgage (re-mortgaging), taking out a second mortgage, or arranging a secured loan.

Second mortgages and secured loans are often used to pay for home improvements or other major purchases. However, some homeowners have taken to rolling up their unsecured debts and securing them against their home. This 'mortgage equity withdrawal' is a very dangerous strategy and can backfire horribly if you find it difficult to keep up repayments on your new mortgage. In the worst-case scenario, eating into your housing equity could ultimately lead to you losing the roof over your head.

Stamp Duty Land Tax (SDLT)

When buying a home in the UK, you are highly likely to pay Stamp Duty Land Tax, commonly referred to as 'stamp duty'. This tax is paid only by property buyers, not sellers. Although stamp duty is a fixed percentage of the purchase price, the rates of tax are banded, as shown below:

Purchase price	SDLT rate (%)
*Up to £125,000	Nil
Over £125,000 to £250,000	1%
Over £250,000 to £500,000	3%
Over £500,000	4%

*This limit has been temporarily increased to £175,000 for one year, beginning 3rd September 2008.

It's important to note that the higher rate of tax is payable on the entire purchase price, not just the amount in excess of the previous band. Thus, a house costing £249,999 would attract stamp duty of 1%, or £2499.99. However, a house costing just £2 more would attract tax of 3% of £250,001, or £7500.03. This tax jump explains the clustering of property prices below the £250,000 and £500,000 stamp duty thresholds.

As most homes in the UK now sell for more than £125,000, the government pockets billions of pounds each year from stamp duty. Thus, HM Treasury has been one of the biggest winners during the long housing boom.

Term

Mortgage lenders use the word 'term' to describe the period, or life, of a mortgage. Just like schoolchildren eagerly awaiting the end of the school term, mortgage borrowers look forward to a long holiday when their mortgage term is over!

Valuation and survey fees

Before lending against a property, a mortgage lender needs to be sure that it has decent security for any loan granted. Therefore, mortgage lenders will insist on a valuation or full structural survey being conducted. Usually, the charge for this inspection will be paid by the prospective homeowner. However, a basic valuation may be provided free as part of a mortgage package. Otherwise, you should expect to pay around £250 for a basic survey, £500 for a more detailed homebuyer's report, or as much as £1000 for a full structural survey.

One final word on home owning

In common with our American cousins, we Brits have a peculiar obsession with house prices and home ownership. Seven in 10 (70%) properties in the UK are owner-occupied. Thus, 17.5 million households take an active interest in house prices.

On the other hand, this 'housing mania' is not shared by our counterparts on the Continent. Indeed, over the past decade, house prices have actually fallen in Germany. Between 2001 and 2006, house prices in the eurozone rose by an average of 40%, compared with 90% for the UK in the same period.

It's important to understand that home ownership is not the be-all and end-all of everything. Likewise, when house prices are out of kilter, renting can be a much cheaper option. Don't believe the housing cheer-leaders who blindly declare that 'renting is dead money'. At certain times, renting can be more financially advantageous than buying.

> **" home ownership is not the be-all and end-all of everything "**

Of course, when house prices are falling, tenants can sit on the sidelines and avoid losing money. Also, it can make sense to rent a home when the ongoing cost of buying far outweighs that of renting. For example, why pay £1500 a month to buy a house when prices are flat or falling, when you can pay £1000 to rent it?

In summary, our national obsession with house prices may in itself lead to unstoppable booms and busts. Basic economics demonstrates that house prices cannot defy financial gravity and keep rising forever. Otherwise, housing costs would eventually consume all of our take-home pay. Therefore, it is highly unlikely that future house prices will rise at anything like the rate seen in the latest boom. In any event, falling or slowly rising house prices may help to restore some sanity to the British housing market!

So, before diving in and buying a house, do your homework first. Work out how much you expect to pay in upfront and ongoing costs, and then balance this against the corresponding costs of renting. For many people, particularly those on the fringes of affordability, the risks and rewards of home ownership simply don't stack up, and these folk would be better off as tenants.

On the other hand, buying and owning a home may well prove to be the most profitable financial decision you make in your life. What's more, do this properly and you won't have to worry about excessive housing costs when you retire from work!

Being a smarter saver

A land fit for lenders

As revealed in the previous chapter, the UK is now a domain dominated by debt. Total personal debt (including mortgages) reached £1448 billion in July 2008. This is almost three times the £500 billion owed when Labour took office in May 1997. With 48 million adults in the UK, this means that the average debt (including mortgages) is just over £30,000 per person!

Furthermore, while personal debt has soared, savings levels have plummeted. One way to measure our enthusiasm for saving is to study the *savings ratio*. This measures the proportion of our take-home pay which we save as a nation. The bad news is that putting spare cash aside has become deeply unfashionable.

Rising house prices and the savings slump

In 1992, the UK savings ratio was riding high at 11.7%. In other words, 16 years ago, we saved almost one pound in eight of our take-home pay. By the first quarter of 2008, this ratio had collapsed to 1.1%, or just one pound in 90 pounds. This is the lowest savings ratio recorded since 1959, when Britain was still coping with post-war hardship.

One reason why saving has suffered such a severe setback is the 'wealth effect' caused by rising house prices. Across the UK as a whole, house prices rose every year from 1996 to 2007. This 12-year winning streak enriched homeowners to the tune of trillions of pounds. Thus, backed by this new-found wealth, they slashed their savings contributions, abandoning the caution shown by their parents and grandparents.

On the other hand, there is some evidence to suggest saving may soon be back on the menu. As house prices start to weaken, the savings ratio should begin to creep up. Indeed, if the UK housing market enters a slump, it's quite likely that we'll see a return to good old-fashioned saving.

The big question: why bother saving at all?

❝ Britain has become obsessed with 'keeping up with the Joneses' ❞

It's a sad fact that celebrity-obsessed Britain has become obsessed with 'keeping up with the Joneses'. Of course, this 'live today, pay tomorrow' culture can only last for so long. Eventually, we will come to our senses and realise that, by living the high life on credit, we are stealing from our future selves. Sacrificing our future for short-term enjoyment is no way to build financial security!

In fact, the allure of saving is remarkably simple. By setting aside some money today, we do two things. First, we create a cash cushion to tide us over when times are hard. Second, by earning the highest rates of interest on our spare cash, we ensure that our emergency fund grows over time. Ideally, you should aim to save, say, at least a tenth (10%) of your income in order to cope with whatever life may throw at you. If you can't save this high a proportion of your income, then simply save what you can. In the words of Tesco, 'Every little helps'.

What is saving?

It's important not to confuse saving with investing. In the simplest terms, saving is putting money on deposit, usually in a savings account maintained by a bank or building society. Thus, saving is purely based on cash and the interest which it generates. On the other hand, investing involves making returns by buying assets such as shares, bonds, property and other items. (For more information on investing, see Chapter 6.)

Cash savings have a number of advantages over other asset classes:

1 Cash is the *most liquid* of all assets. In other words, it's extremely easy to put money into and take money out of a savings account. What's more, there's always strong demand for savers' cash as banks seek to attract more money into their coffers.

2 Saving in cash is *safer and more secure* than any form of investing. By handing over your cash to a bank or building society, you know that your underlying capital will not fall in value. What's more, you will earn interest on your balance, at a rate set by the provider. (For the record, there have been no major bank collapses in the UK since the 1860s. Even when the credit crunch claimed Northern Rock in September 2007, the government stepped in to ensure that savers didn't lose a single penny.)

3 Cash has *no or low transaction charges*. When buying other assets, there is always a price to pay, such as transaction charges, fees and purchase taxes. However, a simple savings account will allow you free and easy access to your money without penalty.

4 Thanks to their liquidity, security and reliability, cash savings are useful for building a pot of money for the *short or medium term*. Few other financial products provide cast-iron guarantees that they will deliver the goods on time, when you need them. Then again, over the long term, saving in cash generally produces inferior returns to racier investments such as shares, as I explain later in the book.

So much for the simple joys of saving. Now let's look at the saver's greatest enemies: inflation and the taxman. As Lenin (Vladimir Ilyich Ulyanov; leader of the Russian Revolution) once remarked:

The way to crush the bourgeoisie is to grind them between the millstones of taxation and inflation.

How inflation eats away at your money

The first problem with saving in cash is that, over the long term, your money tends to buy less and less. Thus, as the years go by, a set sum of money is worth less and less. This is because of inflation: the tendency for the price of goods and services to rise over time. As the cost of consumer goods rises, it erodes the value of the money sitting in your savings account.

Here in the UK, we measure inflation using three different indices: the Consumer Prices Index (CPI), the Retail Prices Index (RPI) and the Retail Prices excluding Mortgage Interest Payments Index (RPIX).

The CPI is the index used by the Bank of England's Monetary Policy Committee when setting interest rates (its current target for CPI is 2% a year). The CPI excludes housing costs, but the RPI includes mortgage interest payments, so it more accurately reflects the price pressures faced by homeowners. Lastly, the RPIX includes most housing costs, but ignores mortgage costs, which makes it more stable than the RPI.

In post-war Britain, inflation has varied enormously from year to year, depending on the prevailing economic conditions of the time. However, history provides us with no clues as to what level of inflation we face in the years to come, so let's examine the present.

In June 2008, the RPI measure of inflation was 4.6%. What this means is that the 'basket' of goods and services included in the RPI cost £100 in June 2007. However, by June 2008, this basket cost £104.60, or 4.6% more than it did a year earlier. Thus, inflation is a backward-looking measure, and the above indices measure price changes over the previous 12 months.

Conversely, £104.60 in June 2008 has the same 'buying power' as £100 had in June 2007. Thus, £100 in June 2008 has the same 'real' (after inflation) value as £100/1.046 = £95.60 a year earlier. So, thanks to rising prices, your £100 lost £4.40 of value in real terms, after taking RPI at 4.6% into account.

Generally speaking, higher inflation is good news for borrowers, because it reduces the real value of their debts over time. On the other hand, inflation is a menace to savers, because it eats away at their hard-earned cash. In addition, pensioners and people on fixed or slowly rising incomes are hit hard by inflation. Indeed, even modest levels of inflation can seriously undermine the value of your money, especially over long periods of time.

Take a look at the following table, which shows how the value of £100 shrinks over time, thanks to various levels of inflation:

The real value of £100 over time, after inflation

Yearly rate	5	10	15	20	25
1%	£95.15	£90.53	£86.13	£81.95	£77.98
2%	£90.57	£82.03	£74.30	£67.30	£60.95
3%	£86.26	£74.41	£64.19	£55.37	£47.76
4%	£82.19	£67.56	£55.53	£45.64	£37.51
5%	£78.35	£61.39	£48.10	£37.69	£29.53

As you can see, with yearly inflation of 5%, £100 in today's terms will more than halve in value after 15 years. In fact, its real value will be just £48.10. This means that it has lost 52% of its buying power over one and a half decades. Hence, over long periods, even modest levels of inflation can do major damage to your spending power.

The simple way to counter inflation is to make sure that the interest rate earned by your savings exceeds inflation each year. However, this is not always possible, and there is always the possibility that inflation could shrink your savings in any given year ahead. One guaranteed way to beat inflation is to buy Index-linked Savings Certificates from National Savings & Investments (NS&I). We look at these and other NS&I savings accounts later in this chapter.

Alas, inflation isn't the only worry which savers face, because HM Revenue & Customs (HMRC, alias 'the taxman') is lurking in the wings, as always.

How the taxman claims his cut

If your total earnings (including income, savings interest, dividends, etc.) are sufficiently low that they fall below the tax-free personal allowance, then you do not have to pay tax on your savings interest. For adults under 65, this allowance is £6000 for the 2008/09 tax year.

Thus, as a non-taxpayer, you do not need to pay tax on your savings interest. Normally, a fifth (20%) of your savings interest is automatically deducted at source and paid to HMRC by your savings provider. If you are a non-taxpayer, then you can reclaim this tax and avoid future tax by asking your bank or building society for a form R85. You then complete and return this form to stop tax being deducted from your savings interest at source.

If your total earnings fall below the threshold for higher-rate tax (roughly £41,500 in 2007/08), then you are a basic-rate taxpayer. Thus, you lose a fifth (20%) of your savings interest to HM Revenue & Customs. In other words, if your gross interest rate (the before-tax rate) is 5% a year, then your net interest (after tax) will be 4%.

If your total earnings exceed the higher-rate threshold, then you pay twice as much tax on your savings. Instead of paying 20% tax, you hand over 40% to HMRC. The first 20% is deducted at source and the second 20% is collected via your annual tax return or by adjustments to your tax code. Hence, a rate of 5% a year becomes a mere 3% after paying higher-rate tax.

The best way to avoid paying tax on savings is to make use of a hugely popular tax-free savings account known as a cash ISA (Individual Savings Account). These are open to UK residents aged 16 or over and are explained in more detail later in this chapter.

Summing up: tax and inflation together

Taken together, tax and inflation can have a devastating effect on the long-term value of cash savings. Take, for example, higher-rate taxpayers earning 5% a year on their savings. After 40% tax, their interest rate plunges to just 3%. Furthermore, after accounting for inflation at (say) 4%, they actually make a negative return (–1%) on their savings. Thus, unless you take steps to minimise the effect of tax and inflation, your savings stash could shrink over time!

Choosing a savings account

Having established the pros and cons of stashing cash, let's now establish what we need to consider when choosing a specific savings account. Quite simply, you need to bear in mind these five factors:

1   The *interest rate* – the higher, the better. Bear in mind that some accounts pay 'tiered' rates of interest, so the higher your balance, the higher the rate your entire pot earns.

2   How much *access* you have to your money. The most flexible accounts offer 'instant access', usually via a cashcard or passbook. The next step up is 'easy access' or 'no notice' accounts, which usually allow you to withdraw money via the banking payments system. If you're willing to keep your hands off your cash for long periods, then accounts with notice periods and withdrawal penalties come into play. There's more about these accounts later.

3   Whether the account comes with *strings attached*. Ideally, you should aim to combine high rates of interest with no-strings access to your cash. However, by agreeing to lock away your money or restrict withdrawals, you may be able to enhance your returns even further.

4   Whether you plan to *save regularly* or deposit a *lump sum*. Most accounts allow you to make one-off deposits, however large they are (some accounts will hold up to £2 million). Then again, by saving monthly, you can access the very highest rates of interest on offer.

5 Whether you can take advantage of *'special' savings accounts*. In their ongoing search for savers, banks and building societies are always coming up with 'niche' accounts. These are designed to appeal to a particular target market, such as older savers.

How secure are your savings?

What would be a saver's worst nightmare? My guess is that having saved carefully over a period of years, savers suddenly see their nest eggs spectacularly wiped out when a bank collapses. Indeed, the huge queues outside Northern Rock branches in mid-September 2007 clearly demonstrated the public's lack of confidence in the banking system.

Just to be clear, all UK-authorised banks, including UK divisions of foreign banks, belong to a safety net known as the Financial Services Compensation Scheme (FSCS). This independent, statutory body is funded by a levy on financial firms, and provides guarantees to savers and investors. If a financial institution gets into trouble and is unable, or likely to be unable, to pay claims against it, then the FSCS steps in as a 'fund of last resort'.

As far as savers are concerned, the FSCS guarantees the first £35,000 of savings in any single institution. Of course, for joint accounts, this protection is doubled to £70,000. Thus, if you're a cautious individual with more than £35,000 of savings, then you may feel safer spreading your savings across several different institutions.

However, it's *vital* to understand that this protection applies per institution. Hence, you must check to see if different banks are part of the same registration with the Financial Services Authority (FSA). For example, the single registration for banking giant HBOS includes the following banks: Bank of Scotland, Birmingham Midshires, Halifax, Intelligent Finance, Saga and the AA. Likewise, Lloyds TSB and Cheltenham & Gloucester count as a single institution, and so on.

Hence, it pays to know your banking brands before spreading your cash around!

(By the way, now that the government has nationalised Northern Rock, it now guarantees all deposits in the bank. Thus, Northern Rock is now as 'rock solid' as the government's own piggybank, National Savings & Investments!)

*The attempted takeover of HBOS by Lloyds TSB, announced on 17 September 2008 may affect these banks' FSCS registrations, so do check before investing.

Savings accounts in more detail

Before you decide on a home for your spare cash, it's worth getting to know the savings market in more detail. Indeed, only by getting to grips with the world of savings accounts can you find the account that is ideal for you. So, let's take a look at the vast range of savings accounts on offer (in alphabetical order).

Accounts for older savers

In the UK, adults aged over 50 account for a third of the population, which comes to 20 million people. However, these 'silver' savers own around three-quarters (75%) of all UK wealth, according to a 2007 survey by Abbey, with assets worth £5.2 trillion of the total £6.9 trillion.

Naturally, savings providers are extremely keen to capture a slice of senior savers' spare cash. In order to do this, they have created a range of savings accounts aimed exclusively at the over-fifties or over-sixties. Clearly, this market is booming: in mid-2007, *Moneyfacts* magazine listed 83 different savings accounts aimed at the over-fifty market.

Given that many of these over-fifties acounts pay impressive rates of interest, it's not surprising that several appear in the Best Buy tables. However, my advice would be to weigh up these savings accounts in the same way as you would any other account.

Indeed, many accounts for senior savers pay mediocre rates of interest, so these should be rejected as second-rate gimmicks.

Cash Individual Savings Accounts (ISAs)

The Cash ISA should be considered the bedrock of any taxpayer's savings strategy. The reason for this is simple: cash ISAs pay *tax-free interest* which doesn't have to be declared to the taxman. Given their tax-favoured status, it's no surprise that cash ISAs are hugely popular: 20 million people have one or more cash ISA accounts.

Of course, there are limits on how much tax the government is willing to miss out on, so there are limits on cash ISAs:

1   They are open only to UK residents aged 16 and over.

2   There is an annual limit on contributions, which is £3600 for the 2008/09 tax year.

3   If you pay the maximum £3600 into a cash ISA and then make a withdrawal, this money cannot be put back into the same ISA. Instead, you will have to wait until the next tax year begins on 6 April, when you can open a new ISA. Of course, you can continue paying into your existing ISA, but it makes sense to shop around for the best rates each year before doing so.

Other than the above restrictions, cash ISAs operate in much the same way as ordinary savings accounts. So, look for a high rate of interest, keep an eye on this rate, and be prepared to transfer your cash ISAs to another provider to chase the highest rates.

Child Trust Funds (CTFs)

In a nutshell, the Child Trust Fund is a tax shelter for the under-eighteens. CTFs were launched by the government in 2005 in order to encourage parents, relatives and friends to save more for children. All babies born after 31 August 2002 are entitled to have a CTF and, to help things along, the state chips in.

When a child is born and its parents claim Child Benefit, HM Revenue & Customs automatically sends a voucher to the parent, usually the mother. Most children receive a gift of £250; for low-income families, this is doubled to £500. The intention is for a second voucher of equal value to be handed over when the child reaches seven, but this will not happen before 1 September 2009 at the earliest.

Parents can choose from three types of Child Trust Fund:

■ a tax-free cash savings account;

■ a stakeholder equity account (which allows investment into various stock-market funds with charges limited to 1.5% a year); and

■ a non-stakeholder equity account (which allows parents to choose individual shares on behalf of their child). The charges for these accounts depend on the provider used, but are broadly in line with those levied by shares ISAs (see Chapter 6).

The real benefit of a Child Trust Fund is that parents, grandparents, other relatives and friends can together contribute up to £1200 a year. This can continue every year until the child reaches 18, when the CTF matures. At this point, the child can withdraw his/her savings, or roll them over into another tax-free shelter similar to an ISA.

What's more, you can transfer a CTF to another provider at any time, without charge. Thus, you could start off with a cash CTF and then transfer it to a stock market CTF later down the line. It's critical to note that children get full access to their CTF on reaching their eighteenth birthday. This could be a problem, especially if your child decides to splurge the cash, instead of spending it wisely. Nevertheless, CTFs are a great way to save for a child's future, encourage the savings habit and promote financial education.

However, it's my view that saving in cash for a period of 18 years is not the best use of a CTF. Indeed, over any 18-year period in the past four decades, the stock market has outperformed cash. Therefore, I'd encourage parents to use CTFs for share-based investing, while building up cash savings for children elsewhere. However, if you want to track down the Best Buys for cash CTFs, then visit *www.moneyfacts.co.uk* for the latest deals.

Finally, for more information on CTFs, visit the government website at www.childtrustfund.gov.uk.

Children's savings accounts

❝ like adults, children have their own personal tax allowance ❞

It's not widely known that, like adults, children have their own personal tax allowance. For the 2008/09 tax year, this comes to £6000. Thus, a child can earn up to £6000 before paying tax on his/her income.

Alas, there is a limit on how much savings interest a child can earn from capital gifted by a parent. Currently, this stands at £100 per parent, so that's £200 from two parents. Any interest earned above this threshold is liable to tax at the parent's highest rate – which could be up to 40%. On the other hand, interest earned from gifts from relatives other than parents doesn't fall into this £100 trap, so granny and grandad can be as generous as they wish!

To put the £100 rule into context, let's assume that a child has a savings account which pays interest of 5% a year. To earn £200 a year, the youngster would have to have £4000 on deposit, which is beyond the reach of most parents. In order for your child's interest to be paid tax free, you must complete and submit a form R85 to the bank or building society.

Again, the golden rule for children's savings account is to maximise your rate of interest while minimising the strings attached. Finally, don't be tempted by free gifts and other gimmicks on offer, or accounts promoted by cartoon characters or celebrities. By choosing the best-paying account, your child will thank you further down the line!

Everyday/easy-access/no-notice savings accounts

It makes good sense to have a 'cash cushion' to fall back on when times get tough. My advice would be to keep between three and 12 months' living expenses (how much you need to live on, which should be less than your take-home pay) in a savings account which lets you get at your cash when you need to. In other words, keep your rainy-day money, emergency fund or nest egg in an easy-access or no-notice account. You can avoid tax by keeping your emergency fund in a cash ISA, but you may not be able to replace money previously withdrawn.

These are the everyday, common-or-garden accounts on which tens of millions of savers rely. An ideal easy-access account should pay a great rate of interest, while allowing you to make unlimited withdrawals without penalty. In addition, it should pay a good ongoing rate over time, so be wary of accounts which pay short-term introductory accounts in order to boost the rate for, say, six months. Also, watch out for sneaky rate cuts, and be prepared to move your money if your rate is no longer up to scratch.

First-class names; second-class returns

One marketing trick widely used by savings providers is to give saving accounts fancy-sounding names. For example, you can find accounts which come with the following, supposedly reassuring, labels: Diamond, Emerald, Gold, Midas, Premium and Super. Although these names give the impression of being valuable or upmarket, the reality is usually different. A pig with a posh name is still a pig, so don't be fooled by these 'grand brands'!

Fixed-rate savings accounts

It's important to understand that the vast majority of savings accounts pay variable rates of interest. In other words, the rates on offer can rise and fall over time, depending on the general interest-rate environment and the provider's strategy. Then again, many savers (particularly those who rely on their savings to supplement their income) prefer to enjoy a solid, predetermined rate of interest. This is where fixed-rate savings accounts and bonds come in.

As you'd imagine, a fixed-rate savings account does exactly what it says on the tin: your rate is fixed for a specific period of time. Typically, savings providers are looking for savers willing to tie up their money for six months to two years, although fixes of up to five years are available. In return for putting their money in handcuffs, savers demand tasty rates of interest. Thus, fixed-rate accounts can provide market-beating returns. Indeed, the best interest rates can exceed two percentage points above the Bank of England's base rate. With the base rate at 5% in the summer of 2008, the best fixed-rate savings accounts paid 7%+ a year before tax.

However, before tying up your money in this way, think carefully. Make sure that you have enough cash salted away elsewhere before committing all of your savings to a fixed-rate deal. Otherwise, you may not have access to your savings in an emergency, or may have to pay a steep penalty for doing so. Also, if you fix your rate and general interest rates rise then you could lose out, so you should form a view on where you expect prevailing rates to go in the immediate future.

Guaranteed income bonds (GIBs)

Guaranteed income bonds are not savings accounts as such. However, they are a popular alternative to the traditional savings account, especially among retired savers. GIBs are issued by insurance companies, rather than banks or building societies. They pay a fixed rate of interest and guarantee to return your capital in full when the term is up and the bond matures. In most cases, these bonds run for periods from one to five years, providing security of income and capital over long periods.

GIBs have a tax advantage over traditional savings accounts, because they pay interest net of basic-rate tax. Thus, basic-rate (20%) taxpayers are not required to pay tax on interest from GIBs. However, higher-rate (40%) taxpayers are liable to further tax and must declare this income on their tax return.

This example shows how this tax benefit works (taken from a one-year GIB issued in 2007):

Rate net of basic-rate tax (% AER)	Gross equivalent for basic-rate taxpayer (% AER)	Gross equivalent for higher-rate taxpayer (% AER)
4.72	5.90	6.29

So, a basic-rate taxpayer would receive yearly interest of 4.72% with no further tax to pay. This is the same as earning 5.90% a year in a taxable savings account, because 5.90% less 20% tax is 4.72%. For higher-rate taxpayers receiving 4.72% interest would have to pay 20% of this to the taxman. Thus, they would receive only 3.78% after tax. For them, this is the equivalent of 6.29% a year, because 6.29% less 40% tax is 3.78%.

Lastly, if you are interested in buying GIBs, then it makes sense to consult a specialist adviser before buying. Firms such as www.baronworth.co.uk can find you the best rates and negotiate enhancements to improve your returns.

Monthly or annual interest?

Most savings accounts pay annual interest, so you receive your interest once a year, usually on the anniversary of opening your account. However, some accounts do give you the option of having your interest paid monthly. This is a useful option for pensioners and other savers who rely on a regular income from their savings to help meet their living expenses.

Of course, if you withdraw your interest each month, then you won't benefit from compounding, whereby your interest earns further interest, and this interest earns yet more interest, and so on. Also, paying monthly interest adds more costs for banks. Thus, in every case, the monthly interest paid will be slightly lower than its yearly equivalent.

when comparing savings accounts, always check the gross rate *and* the AER

Incidentally, every savings account must show its Annual Equivalent Rate (AER). This provides a benchmark which enables savers to compare the yearly value of the interest paid. So, when comparing savings accounts, always check the gross rate (the rate before tax) *and* the AER, to see its annual equivalent.

National Savings & Investments (NS&I): 100% secure

NS&I is backed by HM Treasury and is used to provide extra funds to support government spending. As this particular piggybank enjoys the 'full faith and credit of HM Government', it is usually described as 'a 100% safe place for your money'. Indeed, NS&I has around £83 billion of savers' money, making it one of the UK's leading savings providers.

Thanks to its government-sponsored status, NS&I has a broad and unique range of savings products. As well as offering cash ISAs and traditional, taxable savings accounts, it offers several tax-free savings accounts aimed at savers young and old.

The table below summarises NS&I's five most popular products.

I'm quite a fan of the Index-linked and Fixed Interest Savings Certificates, because these earn tax-free returns over pre-set periods, while guaranteeing both your interest and your original deposits. On the other hand, I'm not particularly taken with Children's Bonus Bonds and Income Bonds, as there are better alternatives available elsewhere.

As for Premium Bonds, they are, in effect, a gamble. You have a microscopic chance of winning a million, but are far more likely to win one of the smaller prizes of £50 or £100. Then again, if you hold a large number of bonds and enjoy average luck, then you should earn close to the advertised return (currently 3.60% a year). For higher-rate taxpayers, this is the equivalent of 6% a year before tax. This is a tidy return, which explains the popularity of Premium Bonds among the well-heeled. With a lot of money, you can win!

I have not included interest rates for these products, as they can change several times a year. However, you can find these and other information about NS&I's savings range at *www.nsandi.com*.

Account name	Description
Fixed Interest Savings Certificates	Lump-sum investments which earn guaranteed rates of tax-free interest over set periods, currently two or five years. The minimum purchase is £100 and the maximum is £30,000 (£15,000 in the two-year issue and the same in the five-year issue). Anyone aged 7+ can invest; certificates can also be bought on behalf of under-7s.
Index-linked Savings Certificates	Lump-sum investments which earn guaranteed rates of tax-free interest that match inflation, as measured by the Retail Prices Index (RPI), plus extra interest on top. Thus, these certificates are guaranteed to keep ahead of general inflation. The minimum purchase is £100 and the maximum is £30,000 (£15,000 in the three-year issue and the same in the five-year issue). Because inflation fluctuates, you don't know exactly how much you will receive until your certificates mature. Cashing in early will reduce your returns. Anyone aged 7+ can invest; certificates can also be bought on behalf of under-7s.
Premium Bonds	Monthly prize draws give you the chance of winning tax-free cash prizes. If you don't win anything, then your return that month is zero. There are around 1.7 million prizes, ranging from £50 to two £1 million jackpots. The more bonds you own, the greater your chance of winning. The total awards paid by the prize fund are equivalent to a yearly interest rate of 3.60%. The chance of a single bond winning any prize is one in 21,000. Available to anyone who is 16+; parents and grandparents can buy bonds for children. The minimum purchase is £100 and the maximum is £30,000.
Children's Bonus Bonds	A savings bond for children which pays a guaranteed rate of tax-free interest. Anyone aged 16+ can invest for anyone under 16 in the child's name. These bonds pay a fixed rate of interest for five years and can continue until the child's 21st birthday. All returns are tax free for both child and adult.
Income Bonds	These lump-sum bonds pay a monthly income while your money is invested. The interest rate is variable and is paid gross (without tax being deducted). However, taxpayers will be liable for tax on this interest. You have easy access to your money with no notice and no penalties. The minimum purchase is £500 and the maximum is £1 million. Anyone aged 7+ can invest; bonds can also be bought on behalf of under-7s.

Notice accounts

With a notice account, you do not have immediate access to your money. Instead, you agree to tie up your money in return for higher rates of interest. For instance, a 90-day notice account means that you must give 90 days' notice of your intention to make a withdrawal. If you are unable to do this, then the usual penalty is to forfeit the interest that would otherwise be earned over the notice period (in this case, 90 days).

Notice periods for these accounts are as short as seven days and as long as a year or more. Although it can be a good idea to limit your access to some of your cash, I'm not a fan of 'having your money in handcuffs'. Indeed, given that Best Buy no-notice accounts offer superior rates to almost all notice accounts, there's little to be gained by tying up your money.

Offshore savings accounts

British banks constantly wage war on each other in an attempt to win the largest possible share of the savings market. As a result, savers in the UK have thousands of accounts from which to choose. However, this battle extends beyond the UK, as foreign banks and offshore arms of UK banks are keen to attract savers.

Given the panic induced by the near-collapse of Northern Rock, British savers are becoming increasingly reluctant to send their savings to banks beyond these shores. Hence, offshore savings account resort to offering headline-grabbing rates of interest in order to snare savers. This seems to work, as around three million UK residents have offshore accounts, with total deposits of £180 billion.

❝ you do not enjoy the same level of consumer protection when you squirrel your nuts offshore! ❞

Generally speaking, most offshore accounts promoted in the UK are based in Guernsey, Jersey or the Isle of Man – all well-known tax havens. However, you should understand that you do not enjoy the same level of consumer protection when you squirrel your nuts offshore! Also, it is illegal to hide off-shore interest earnings from HM Revenue & Customs. Hence, the taxman conducts high-profile campaigns to grab its fair share of the tax due on this overseas income.

Then again, some offshore accounts allow you to 'defer' interest indefinitely, until you decide to bring back your money to the mainland. In effect, no interest is earned until you repatriate your money, at which point you declare this interest to HMRC and pay any tax due.

Thus, an offshore account allows you to roll up your interest off-shore and only pay tax when you repatriate your deposit. This can be useful if you expect to pay a lower rate of tax in the future. For example, when you retire, your tax rate might drop from 40% to 20%, thanks to a lowering of your income.

To me, saving offshore is a big leap of faith – you need to be absolutely sure about the security and financial strength of an offshore bank before parting with your cash. On the whole, the depositor protection provided by the Financial Services Compensation Scheme (FSCS) in the UK is superior to offshore safety nets.

For the record, there is *no depositor protection whatsoever* in Guernsey and Jersey. In the Isle of Man, your money is covered by a scheme under the Banking Business (Compensation of Depositors) Regulation 1991. However, this protection is limited, as only three-quarters (75%) of the first £20,000 of savings with an institution is covered, so the maximum payout is £15,000.

So, before handing over your savings to an offshore bank, ask what depositor protection applies, what an offshore bank's credit rating is, and whether an offshore subsidiary is guaranteed by a UK-based parent. Otherwise, your money could sink without trace into the sea!

Rate guarantees

Some accounts which offer market-beating rates of interest also come with an additional benefit in the form of a rate guarantee. For example, they promise that the rate will not fall below the Bank of England base rate until, say, the end of 2009.

Although a rate guarantee can be very reassuring, remember that it only sets a floor on your interest rate during the period in question. Thus, if the guarantee is at a fairly low level, then your interest rate could fall this far, but no further. Treat rate guarantees as a bonus, but keep your eyes on the real prize, which is the actual rate your savings earn.

Regular-savings accounts

Apart from a table-topping cash ISA, nothing beats a regular-savings account. These are ideal for disciplined savers who are prepared to save a monthly sum for at least a year. What's more, there is a huge benefit to be had from committing to saving regularly, as these accounts pay premium rates of interest.

As you'd expect, regular-savings accounts come with strings attached. Typically, you agree to pay a monthly amount of between £10 and £500 by direct debit or standing order for 12 consecutive months. Do this, and you can earn rates which can reach 10% a year. However, if you miss a payment or withdraw any amount, then your interest rate plunges and you lose out.

It helps to think of regular-savings accounts as one-year bonds which pay a fixed rate of interest while you drip-feed in your money. Of course, if you have a lump sum to save, then it makes sense to put it into a top savings account in one go, rather than over a period of months. But a regular-savings account is ideal for saving a proportion of your wage or other income.

TESSA and her friend TOISA

Finally, we come to TESSA: the Tax Exempt Special Savings Account (TESSA). Along with Personal Equity Plans (PEPs) TESSAs were the forerunners of today's ISAs. In short, TESSA was a tax-free savings account into which savers could deposit up to £9000 over its life of five years. TESSA was killed off in April 1999, when ISAs hit the savings scene.

Obviously, the last TESSAs matured in April 2004, five years after they were withdrawn. However, TESSA lives on today, having transformed into TOISA – the TESSA Only ISA. When TESSAs matured, the government allowed savers to place this pot (excluding any interest earned) into a follow-on account known as a TOISA. So, although TESSAs have been withdrawn for almost a decade, they live on today as TOISAs.

The only thing worth knowing about TOISAs is that, as with cash ISAs, you can switch these between savings providers in order to earn the highest rates of interest.

Five steps to splendid saving

Your aim as a saver is to keep your money safe, while making sure that it earns the highest rates of interest. To sum up this chapter, here are five simple tips to help you to achieve this goal:

1 Try to avoid paying tax. Why lose up to 40% of your savings interest to the taxman, when you can save up to £3600 per tax year in a tax-free cash ISA?

2 To earn the highest rates of interest, try setting aside a set amount each month in a regular-savings account.

3 If you need to dip into your savings pot now and again, then don't tie up your money in a notice account.

4 If you don't want to lose out from future rate cuts, then consider locking away your savings in a fixed-rate account.

5 If you are aged over 50, then look into the range of specialist

savings accounts aimed at for senior savers, from the likes of Coventry BS, Heritable Bank and SAGA.

After reading and absorbing this chapter, you should be all set to become a superior saver. Now let's move on to learn how to protect yourself, your family and your prized possessions.

5

Protecting yourself and your assets

I n the first four chapters of this book, we have looked at ways to boost your income and build wealth through better budgeting, spending, borrowing and saving. Now it's time to take a look at what you can do to maintain your lifestyle when times turn tough.

Insurance: a protection racket?

One of the simplest ways to protect yourself, your income, your family and your prized possessions is to buy insurance. In its simplest terms, an insurance policy transfers risk between an insured (that's you) and an insurer (often a large or long-established company). In return for accepting this risk, the insurer charges you a fee, known as an insurance premium. Typically, this premium is collected monthly or yearly for as long as you remain 'on risk'.

Of course, all insurance is a gamble. This is because neither you nor an insurer can be sure whether a claim will arise and, if so, how much it will cost. However, an insurer has access to a huge bank of historic information regarding various risks. Hence, it employs specialist statisticians, known as actuaries, to analyse and interpret these data in order to price its policies accurately.

Sure enough, by pooling risks and premiums from a large group of policyholders, an insurer can be reasonably confident of a

> **❝ just like any other business, an insurer is in the business of making profit ❞**

rewarding outcome. If the actuaries got their sums perfectly right, then the claims paid out plus the insurer's expenses would perfectly balance the premiums collected. However, just like any other business, an insurer is in the business of making profit. It is not interested in a zero-sum game, where it pays out as much as it takes in.

Therefore, an insurer swings the odds in its favour by charging more for its policies than it needs to meet its predicted claims and expenses. This extra profit can then be used to strengthen the insurer's reserves or increase payouts to its shareholders. In summary, the 'insurance equation' looks like this:

$$\text{Premium Charged} = \text{True Risk} + \text{Extra Profit}$$

Insurance has become an unfair gamble

When it comes to taking gambles from the public, an insurer holds ALL the cards. It is expert in accurately assessing and pricing risks. On the other hand, the public is truly *terrible* at understanding both personal risks and statistics. Hence, most of us don't have the first clue whether an insurance policy is a Best Buy, offers 'fair value' or is a complete rip-off!

The bad news is that far too many insurance companies are willing and eager to take advantage of ill-informed customers. By playing on our ignorance, they can charge us several times the 'true' premium and thus pocket mouth-watering profits from what has become an unfair gamble. In addition, they can pack insurance contracts with exclusions, loopholes and get-out clauses in order to reduce the risk of a successful claim.

Thus, after two decades of working for, or writing about, insurance companies, I have reached the conclusion that, by and large, they no longer have the public's best interests at heart. Some insurance industry habits leave a lot to be desired, such as their preference for new over existing customers.

Indeed, I would even go so far as to say that some insurance policies simply aren't worth buying, under any circumstances. These
policies have become so unfair and overpriced that they should
not be considered as insurance at all. Instead, they have become
guaranteed money-making machines, designed to bamboozle
and fleece the public!

Turning 'dead money' into a fair game

Because of its perceived greed, the insurance industry has
acquired a bad name with the public. Many people – fed up with
rejected claims and broken promises – consider insurance policies
to be 'dead money'. Whilst I sympathise with this view, I believe
that there is still a need for insurance in everyday life. All we need
to do is ensure that we buy the right policies at the right price. In
other words, we need to turn insurance back into a fair game
once more.

In summary, our goal as consumers is to decide which insurance
policies we can do without and then reject them. Likewise, when
it comes to laying off the big risks in life, we need to choose the
right cover at a value-for-money price.

Your guide to the insurance jungle

Over the rest of this chapter, I explain and comment on many
different types of insurance which you may encounter in
everyday life. However, when you go into a jungle, it pays to take
an expert guide with you. That's why I'm a fan of insurance
brokers – expert intermediaries who help you to choose insurance and then search some or all of the market on your behalf.

There are thousands of insurance brokers in the UK, of which
around 2500 firms belong to trade association BIBA, the British
Insurance Brokers' Association. You can find a local BIBA member by
using its online search at *www.biba.org.uk/ConsumerHome.aspx*.
(Note that BIBA members only provide advice on general insurance
policies, not life cover.)

Now let's take a look at those different types of insurance, in alphabetical order.

Breakdown (roadside recovery) cover (well worth having)

If you're one of the UK's 33 million motorists, then you should take a look at breakdown insurance. Indeed, the more miles you drive, and the less reliable your vehicle, the more likely you are to need roadside rescue assistance.

Breakdown cover provides help for you to continue your journey or to return home when your car develops a fault and you end up stranded at the roadside. The most basic policy only covers you if your car breaks down away from your home and needs fixing. The next step up, a 'roadside and home rescue' policy, provides assistance if your car fails to start outside of your home, including towing to a local garage.

A premium 'rescue and recovery' policy may offer a courtesy car to enable you to continue on your journey, or provide overnight accommodation while your car is repaired. It may even include repatriation expenses to cover European trips.

The market for breakdown insurance is dominated by four firms: the AA, Britannia Rescue, Green Flag and the RAC. Typically, you can expect to pay between £60 and £250 a year, depending on the service on offer. However, a cheaper 'pay and claim' roadside recovery policy from AutoAid can cost as little as £36 a year. This covers you, rather than your vehicle, and includes free cover for your spouse or partner.

Lastly, rather than relying on breakdown insurance, it makes more sense to keep your car roadworthy and well-maintained. So, before setting off on a long journey, be sure to check your battery, tyres and lights, plus fuel, oil and water levels. After all, you don't want to be stranded at the roadside in the pouring rain, waiting for a recovery vehicle!

For the definitive guide to low-cost breakdown cover, visit *www.moneysavingexpert.com/insurance/roadside-recovery*.

Car/motor insurance (a must)

Sticking with insurance and motorists, next up is motor insurance. If you run a car, motorcycle or other motorised vehicle, then the law requires that you insure it. Thus, motor insurance is the only compulsory insurance cover in the UK.

Motor insurance policies fall into three different categories:

1 *Fully comprehensive* insurance covers damage to your car, plus other vehicles, property and individuals. As the widest form of cover, it is also the most expensive.

2 *Third party, fire and theft* (TPFT) insurance is a step down from fully comprehensive insurance, because it does not cover damage to your vehicle when you are at fault. However, it does cover fire, theft and vandalism to your vehicle.

3 *Third party insurance* only covers damage to other vehicles, property and individuals. This is the minimum cover allowed in law, and the cheapest, because damage to your vehicle is not covered.

How much you pay for motor insurance depends on the cover you choose, plus a large number of risk factors. These include various personal and motoring characteristics, such as:

■ your claims history (too many 'at fault' claims could see you turned down for cover);

■ your no-claims discount (how long it has been since you made a claim; this discount ranges from 30% for one claim-free year up to 70% after five or more 'clean' years);

■ where you live (premiums are bumped up for high-risk areas);

■ your occupation (some careers involve more driving than others);

■ your age (young men pay the highest premiums);

■ your state of health (a serious medical condition could impair your ability to drive);

■ your gender (because men have more accidents than women);

- your yearly mileage; and
- the make and model of your car (each vehicle falls into a numbered insurance category, based on its value and performance).

Other factors which influence your premium include the excess which you agree to pay (how much of a claim you will bear), and whether or not you choose to insure your no-claims discount. Of course, different insurers place different weights on each of these variables, which makes shopping around for motor insurance a must.

Despite the huge growth in price-comparison websites for insurance, no single broker or website searches the entire market for motor insurance. Nevertheless, searching the five top motor insurance websites will give you quotes from almost all of the UK's leading brokers and insurers.

For a comprehensive guide to tracking down a Best Buy motor insurance, visit *www.moneysavingexpert.com/insurance/compare-cheap-car-insurance.*

Critical illness cover (better options are available)

Critical illness cover pays out a tax-free lump sum if you are diagnosed with one of a number of serious illnesses or conditions. This list of medical problems varies from policy to policy, but will include cancer, coronary artery bypass graft, heart attack, kidney failure, major organ transplant, multiple sclerosis, permanent total disability and stroke.

The premiums you pay will depend on the level of cover chosen, the life of the policy (in years), your age, gender, occupation, smoker status and medical history, and whether your premiums are guaranteed (fixed) or reviewable (variable). Many people who buy critical illness cover do so in order to pay off their mortgage if their health takes a turn for the worse.

However, the big problem with this protection is that its definitions are very narrow, so, for example, non-invasive skin cancers and some prostate cancers are not covered. Furthermore, health insurers have a habit of looking for excuses not to pay out, especially when the sum at stake is very large. When you make a claim, your insurer will go over your medical records with a fine toothcomb, looking for any medical history (disclosed or otherwise) which will allow it to reject your claim.

In my view, critical illness cover is too restrictive and too expensive to be useful for most adults. In most cases, you'd be better off buying income protection, which is much more likely to pay out (see below). Then again, for single people with no dependants, critical illness cover is perhaps preferable to life insurance.

Without an expert guide, it would be impossible to trawl through hundreds of different policies in order to choose the one which best suits your needs. Thus, if you do decide to look into critical illness cover, then my advice would be to use a specialist insurance broker such as *www.lifesearch.co.uk*.

Dental insurance (you can live without it)

Finding (and keeping) an NHS dentist can be hard work. Indeed, in some areas, dentists have closed their books to adult patients. This has fuelled the growth in private dentistry, with millions of adults forced to pay for routine dental treatment.

Personally, I've yet to be convinced of the benefits of paying for dental insurance. When insurers force their way between medics and patients, they aim to profit from this relationship. So, before you rush off to buy dental insurance, stop to consider these alternatives:

■ **Find an NHS dentist** by contacting your local primary care trust, calling NHS Direct on 0845 46 47 or visiting *www.nhsdirect.nhs.uk/find/results/index.aspx*.

■ Join your **employer's dental plan**, if it offers this benefit. Your employer may even pay the premiums for you, but you have to pay tax on this benefit. Even if you have to pay the premiums, joining a group scheme will be much cheaper than buying individual cover.

■ **Self-insure** (become your own insurer) by putting aside a monthly sum to pay for dental treatment as the need arises. By doing this, you cut out the middlemen and earn interest on this emergency fund.

■ **Pay as you go**: around three-quarters (75%) of all private dentistry is paid for on a per-visit basis.

In general, dental insurance policies have a limit on how much you can claim each year, and some require you to pay a percentage of treatment costs. Although general dental treatment is covered, as is emergency work, dental insurance policies do not cover cosmetic and orthodontic dentistry, such as veneers or teeth whitening. Also, serious problems such as mouth cancer are not usually covered, as these will require hospital treatment.

However, if you do decide that dental insurance for you, then be sure to shop around to find the right balance between the premiums paid and the cover available. As premiums increase with age, older customers should take extra care when choosing a policy.

The best way to track down a policy is to use an online search engine such as www.moneysupermarket.com/dentalinsurance. However, this service omits a few leading providers, such as market leaders BUPA and Denplan, plus CIGNA, Tesco and WPA. Alternatively, you can enlist the help of a specialist broker such as Medibroker, see *www.medibroker.co.uk/dental.html*.

For more advice on dental insurance and the alternatives (such as 'capitation' or maintenance schemes, which tie you to a particular dentist), read the guide at www.moneysavingexpert.com/insurance/dental-insurance.

Thus, with dental treatment becoming increasingly expensive, it makes sense to take good care of your teeth. Rather than shelling out every month for dental insurance, invest in a better toothbrush, toothpaste and dental floss. As any dentist will tell you, prevention is better than cure!

Finally, a toothy quote from American poet Ogden Nash:

> 'Some tortures are physical
> And some are mental,
> But the one that is both
> Is dental.'

Extended warranties (avoid these rip-offs)

One of the most profitable and, from the consumer's point of view, least attractive insurance policies is the infamous extended warranty. When you buy an electrical appliance, car or other high-value item, the retailer or dealer will be very keen to sell you an extended warranty. This provides extra protection for a product after the manufacturer's guarantee ends. (Note that some extended warranties are service contracts, rather than insurance policies, but the principle remains the same.)

The big problem with extended warranties is that they are hugely expensive. For example, a two-year extended warranty might add £150 to the cost of a £450 camcorder. In other words, this particular warranty adds a third (33%) to the purchase price. Often, the leading electrical chains make higher profits from selling these contracts than they do from flogging domestic appliances.

Although the Competition Commission attempted to clamp down on the extended warranty market in 2005, it remains an outrageous con. Therefore, my advice is never to buy an extended warranty from a retailer or car dealer. You'd be much better off self-insuring or paying for repairs as they arise.

Then again, if you must have this cover, then buy it from a reputable independent provider, such as *www.warrantydirect.co.uk* or *www.warrantyex.co.uk*. Also, you may save money by buying a multi-appliance policy, which covers a number of appliances for a monthly premium.

Home insurance – buildings and contents – (wise buys, if the price is right)

According to the Association of British Insurers, property insurance premiums in the UK totalled £8.5 billion in 2006. This makes property insurance the second-largest market after motor insurance (£10.3 billion). Roughly three-quarters (75%) of British households have contents insurance; the take-up of buildings insurance is lower, at about six in 10 (60%).

Contents insurance protects your household possessions (if you were to remove a property's roof and turn it upside down, what falls out would be the contents). Buildings insurance covers damage to your property's structure by, for example, fire, flood, storms or subsidence.

Buildings insurance

Of the two, buildings insurance is the more essential. As victims of the downpours in England in summer 2007 will confirm, flood damage can cost £25,000+ to repair. As this is the sort of sum that only millionaires wouldn't miss, I consider buildings insurance to be a must for homeowners. (If you are a tenant then the owner will arrange buildings insurance.)

As well as covering your bricks and mortar, buildings insurance also covers permanent fixtures and fittings (such as kitchen and bathroom fixtures), plus your garden shed, garage and items within your property's boundary.

Premiums for buildings insurance can be calculated in several different ways. Bedroom-rated policies work out your premium based on your number of bedrooms, plus the location, type and age of your property. Other policies work out your premium based on the 'sum assured', which is how much it would cost to rebuild your home from scratch. Another option is to pay a premium for unlimited cover, which avoids any complicated calculations.

If you have a mortgage, then your lender will insist on you having buildings insurance. However, it would be a big mistake

❝ your lender will insist on you having buildings insurance ❞ to buy this cover from your mortgage lender, because its premiums will be extremely uncompetitive. Indeed, these policies can cost up to three times as much as their Best Buy rivals!

Contents insurance

Whether or not you need contents insurance depends on how much you have to lose. If your home is crammed with valuables and expensive consumer goods, then it makes sense to insure these assets. On the other hand, if you live a relatively frugal and modest lifestyle, then you may decide to give contents insurance a miss.

Contents insurance covers your possessions against a range of risks, including fire, flood and theft. Some policies also include accidental damage cover as standard, but some insurers charge extra for this. Another optional extra is 'all risks' cover for personal possessions and valuables while away from your home.

Both buildings and contents insurance include various 'excesses' – amounts that you have to contribute towards the cost of a claim. An excess could range from, say, £50 for a theft claim up to £1000+ for a subsidence problem.

Buying buildings and contents cover

When buying buildings and/or contents insurance, you need to tread carefully. Although it may be cheaper to buy a single policy to cover both risks, this is not always the case. Also, never renew your policy each year without first shopping around for a better-value replacement. Insurers have a habit of raising premiums at renewal time, regardless of whether a customer has made a claim.

Also, before buying, make sure that your cover is adequate and that there are no troublesome exclusions or low levels of cover tucked away in the small print. Otherwise, when you come to make a claim, you could be left out of pocket.

The best way to lower your home insurance premiums is to shop around online. The four leading insurance-comparison websites will give you quotes from close to 100% of the key players in this market. To learn how to do this (and get cashback for your custom), visit *www.moneysavingexpert.com/insurance/home-insurance.*

Finally, keeping your property properly maintained and secure will reduce your premiums and make you less likely to make a claim. For example, being security conscious and fitting a burglar alarm, plus approved locks to windows and doors, will lower your premium.

Healthcare cash plans (cheap and cheerful, but frequently pay out more than you pay in)

Although they are a relic from pre-NHS days, healthcare cash plans (HCPs) still have a role to play today. They are designed to help meet the cost of everyday healthcare expenses, such as dental and optical check-ups, NHS prescription costs, physiotherapy and other outpatient treatments, and cash benefits for hospital stays.

Although HCPs are not as comprehensive as private medical insurance (see below), their premiums are relatively modest, yet their payouts can be substantial. Indeed, money-saving expert Martin Lewis reckons that some policies can pay for themselves six times over each year!

In short, healthcare cash plans are policies that can really pay out. For an annual premium of £50, you may be able to claim benefits of £250+. One reason why HCPs offer such good value is that their providers are usually not-for-profit 'provident' societies or charities. Furthermore, the long-established societies are over 150 years old and have substantial assets. This enables them to be more generous to policyholders than rival PLCs can be.

For more advice on choosing a healthcare cash plan, read *www.moneysavingexpert.com/insurance/healthcare-cash-plans*

Income protection (permanent health insurance) (well worth considering)

Income protection provides cover against the financial impact of long-term sickness or injury. In effect, it replaces your income if you are unable to work for an extended period due to an illness or accident.

Although the state provides some support for people suffering long-term sickness absence, these benefits are largely inadequate. Hence, if you are self-employed or an employee without generous company sick pay, then income protection could help prevent financial hardship.

Income protection pays a tax-free monthly benefit after an initial waiting period. This waiting period can range from four to 104 weeks – the shorter the waiting period, the higher your premium. Usually, this monthly benefit continues until you return to work, reach retirement age (either at 60 or 65) or die. Ideally, you should choose a waiting period which fits in with your employer's sick-pay package.

In order to give claimants some incentive to return to work, the maximum payout from an income-protection policy will be capped. Usually, the maximum payout will be restricted to around three-fifths (60%) of your salary before deductions.

Your premiums will be affected by a number of different factors. Your age, gender, occupation and smoking habits all affect the amount you pay. In addition, guaranteed premiums (which are fixed for the life of a policy) will be higher than reviewable premiums (which can rise, say, every five years).

❝ making a claim can be something of a tall order ❞

One problem with income protection is that, in order to weed out malingering and fraudulent claimants, making a claim can be something of a tall order. Also, given the large sums at risk (for example, a payout of £1500 a month adds up to £270,000 over 15 years), insurers are very strict when it comes to their definition of long-term disability. Generally speaking, you must show that you are so ill that you are no longer able to follow your usual occupation.

Generally, the best way to buy income protection is by joining your employer's scheme. Sometimes, employers cover the cost of this cover. Even if you have to pay for this protection, the premiums are likely to be lower than any you could find by shopping around as an individual.

Buying income protection is no easy task, because no two policies are alike when it comes to what they do and do not cover. Indeed, choosing the perfect policy would tax the combined skills of a doctor and a financial guru. Hence, my advice would be to buy this cover via a specialist protection adviser such as *www.lifesearch.co.uk*.

Life insurance (a must for families; useless for childless, single people)

Life insurance is one of the oldest and most established forms of insurance. It's also one of the simplest, as it pays out a tax-free lump sum if you die. However, the difficulty with life insurance is deciding whether you need it, how much cover you need, and where to buy it.

Do you need it?

First things first: you only need life insurance if your death would cause financial hardship to someone else. So, if you are childless and single, then life insurance is of no use to you. On the other hand, if you are married or living as married, or have children who have yet to fly the nest, then you need to look into life insurance.

As life insurance is such a basic product, it is relatively simple to compare policies. However, there are three different types of life insurance:

- Level-term insurance pays out a fixed sum throughout the life of a policy. Thus, a level-term policy for £100,000 over 20 years would pay out £100,000 if you were to die at any point in the next two decades.

■ Decreasing-term insurance (often called mortgage protection) has a payout which reduces over time. Hence, it is ideal for covering the outstanding debt on a repayment mortgage, as this reduces over time thanks to monthly repayments chipping away at the loan. As its payout falls as time goes by, decreasing-term insurance is cheaper than level-term insurance.

■ Whole-of-life insurance has no specific term, as it pays out a set amount whenever you die. Therefore, unlike other life insurance, whole-of-life will not expire before you do, which makes it more expensive than term insurance. Also, part of your monthly premiums is invested over the long term in order to fund your final payout. This investment element helps to cut premiums for this type of insurance. Whole-of-life policies are often used as part of inheritance tax planning, with the payout helping to meet an anticipated inheritance tax bill.

How much cover do you need?

When deciding how much life cover would be appropriate, it is important to look at your existing arrangements. For example, you may already have life cover for an existing mortgage or 'death in service' cover from your employer.

Nevertheless, at the very least, you should have enough life insurance to leave your partner and/or children debt-free (and after paying your funeral expenses). The next step up is to provide a reasonable standard of living for your dependants. One rule of thumb is to have £150,000 of life cover per child, which should be enough to support them until adulthood.

If you are particularly risk-averse, and have plenty of disposable income, then you can boost your life cover to, say, 10 times your before-tax income. However, there is little point in leaving your family with a Lotto-sized jackpot if you die, because big payouts mean big premiums. Thus, for a typical worker earning an average wage of, say, £25,000 a year, life cover of £250,000 should provide a comfortable cash cushion for dependants.

How much you pay for life insurance will depend on a wide range of factors, including your age, gender, occupation, smoking habits, medical history and state of health. Furthermore, the level of cover chosen, the term (length) of your policy, and the type of cover will also have a bearing on your premiums. Let's take a look at how we can bring down the cost of this valuable protection.

Seven tricks to help you get more life cover for less cash

1 Never, ever buy life insurance from your mortgage lender or bank. In most cases, high-street banks and building societies are 'tied agents', which means that your choice of insurer will be severely restricted. Instead, search the entire market by using an independent financial adviser, such as award-winning broker *www.lifesearch.co.uk*.

2 Many couples buy a single policy to cover two people. However, these 'joint life, first death' policies provide only a single payout if either person dies. Buying separate 'his and hers' policies gets two potential payouts for just a few extra pounds each month. What's more, two separate policies are much easier to split up if you do!

3 If you need life insurance to replace your income after your death, then a policy known as 'family income benefit' (FIB) can be cheaper than buying level-term insurance. Instead of paying out a lump sum, FIB pays out a tax-free monthly income for the remaining term of the policy. If you are strapped for cash then FIB can be a useful alternative to traditional life cover.

4 Inheritance tax (IHT) is a bill which arrives after you depart. In theory, the taxman can grab two-fifths (40%) of your estate above the nil-rate band for IHT, which is £312,000 in the 2008/09 tax year. To avoid this once-in-a-lifetime tax, you should put life insurance policies into trust. This keeps payouts from life insurance separate from your estate, avoids IHT, and speeds up your claim.

5 Although your spouse or partner may not work, his/her contribution to the upkeep of the family home has major

financial value. Indeed, the cost of replacing a stay-at-home parent could amount to £25,000 a year. So, although someone may not a breadwinner, this doesn't mean that they don't need life insurance. If losing your other half would mean hard times for you or your family, then make sure that your partner is covered also.

6 Give up the evil weed. Smoking is a killer, which explains why life insurance premiums for smokers are about half as much again (50% higher) than those for non-smokers. One year after quitting, you should be able to pay the same premium as a non-smoker. Likewise, losing weight or taking other steps to improve your health can also save you money when buying insurance.

7 If you know exactly which policy you need, then try using a 'discount broker' to trim your premiums to the bone. These brokers sacrifice or share their commission with you in order to reduce your premiums. Leading firms include www.cavendishonline.co.uk, *www.moneyworld.com* and *www.life-insurance-online.co.uk.*

In summary, life insurance provides valuable peace of mind, but only to those who really need it and have shopped around to ensure that they have Best Buy cover.

Make a will

Although a will is not strictly an insurance policy, it does provide similar peace of mind. Without a will, your estate will be divided according to intestacy law, making it a hostage of the legal system. However, by making a will, you can ensure that your worldly goods are divided up according to your wishes. Don't use an off-the-shelf will-writing service. Instead, consult a member of the Society of Trust and Estate Practitioners (STEP). You can find a STEP member at *www.step.org.*

Payment protection insurance (the UK's biggest insurance scandal!)

Payment protection insurance (PPI) covers the repayments on your credit card, mortgage, personal loan or other finance agreement if you are unable to work due to an accident, sickness or unemployment. Life cover is also included, except for mortgage PPI. Usually, PPI payouts start when you've been off work for a month and continue each month until you return to work or a total of 12 monthly benefits have been paid.

By my reckoning, there are more than 25 million PPI policies in existence. This makes PPI one of the most widely held insurance policies in the UK. Alas, the big problem with payment protection insurance is that lenders have a stranglehold over this market. With a captive audience to feed on, lenders charge as much as they possibly can for PPI. This lack of competition means that borrowers pay sky-high premiums for this cover. Indeed, my estimate is that lenders and insurers pocket more than £4 billion a year from selling this overpriced rubbish.

> **" lack of competition means that borrowers pay sky-high premiums for this cover "**

PPI is optional cover, which means that it should always be sold on an 'opt in', rather than an 'opt out', basis. Despite this, these policies are frequently sold using high-pressure sales techniques. Indeed, PPI may have been added to your loan without your knowledge, using a dodgy technique known as an 'assumptive sale'.

In February 2007, the Office of Fair Trading referred the PPI market to the Competition Commission. In June 2008, the Commission's report found that the PPI market was essentially anti-competitive. Furthermore, the Financial Services Authority has identified problems at several PPI providers, causing it to hand out fines totalling more than £3 million. Nevertheless, until financial regulators crackdown on PPI mis-selling, this scandal will continue.

To cut a long story short, you should *never* buy PPI when taking out a credit or store card, car or personal loan, mortgage or other finance agreement. Otherwise, you may find that this insurance bumps up the cost of your credit by up to 35%!

Instead of blindly buying PPI, check to see what your employer offers if you are off sick or are made redundant. If you have a comfortable cash cushion in the form of a savings pot or emergency fund, then you may decide that you can live with the risk of illness or job loss. Also, you should find that an income-protection policy (see above) offers similar sickness insurance at a much lower cost.

Finally, there is a growing market for stand-alone payment protection insurance offered by independent providers. In some cases, these policies can be a tenth of the price of those sold on the high street. Best Buy firms for PPI include *www.britishinsurance.com*, *www.bestinsurance.co.uk*, *www.antinsurance.co.uk* and *www.money-supermarket.com/insurance*.

Pet insurance (you can live without it)

As there is no NHS for animals, if your pet becomes ill or is injured then it's up to you to pay any treatment costs. The bad news is that vet's bills can amount to hundreds, or even thousands, of pounds. Hence the existence of pet insurance, which is a bit like private medical insurance (see below) for animals.

According to insurer Norwich Union, there are 14 million cat and dog owners in the UK. Although one in three pets requires medical treatment each year, just one in 10 pets is covered by pet insurance.

Pet insurance for dogs is more expensive than cover for cats, with pedigree breeds attracting the highest premiums. Generally, your yearly premium will rise as your pet gets older and treatment becomes more likely. Also, premiums tend to be higher in cities, particularly in London and the South East.

As well as covering unexpected medical bills, pet insurance also covers you for legal fees for damage caused by your pet. Some policies also pay benefits towards advertising fees and a reward if your pet is lost or stolen. However, these policies do not cover routine treatments, such as vaccinations and neutering. As with all insurance policies, there are maximum limits on payouts per treatment or per year, plus a policy excess of £25 to £100 per claim.

Personally, I wouldn't bother with pet insurance. Instead, I'd set up a 'pet emergency pot', funded by saving, say, £20 a month. However, if you think pet insurance could be worthwhile for your 'family friend', then try the quotation service at *www.moneysupermarket.com/petinsurance* and try leading pet insurer Petplan at *www.petplan.co.uk*.

Private medical insurance (a luxury item)

Although the National Health Service provides comprehensive medical care which is free at the point of use, some NHS services are under considerable strain. Thus, if you have a medical problem which is neither acute (short term and curable) nor life-threatening, then you could face a long waiting list for treatment.

The last thing an ill person needs is a lengthy wait for treatment, which explains why more than six million people are covered by private medical insurance (PMI). This cover enables policyholders to avoid NHS waiting lists, be treated for non-urgent conditions, and enjoy a private room and better hospital food.

Generally speaking, private medical insurance covers the costs associated with outpatient and inpatient care. This includes surgeons' and anaesthetists' fees, accommodation and nursing costs, medication, diagnostic tests and so on.

It's important to understand that PMI only covers acute problems, not chronic (incurable) conditions. Also, emergency treatment is not covered, as this is the job of the NHS. What's more, the quality of treatment in the private sector is no better than that offered by the NHS. Indeed, most private consultants also work in the NHS.

Of course, as with all insurance policies, there are limitations to this cover. Pre-existing medical conditions (problems you had before taking out a policy) are usually excluded, as are self-inflicted injuries, alcoholism and drug use, fertility treatment and normal pregnancy, and cosmetic surgery. Furthermore, there is little or no cover for chronic conditions such as asthma, diabetes, HIV/AIDS and multiple sclerosis.

One good point about private medical insurance is that it pays out a surprisingly large proportion of the premiums charged. Indeed, payouts exceed three-quarters (75%) of the amount collected. However, private medicine remains an expensive business, with treatment costs rising steeply each year. Hence, yearly premiums for a quality PMI policy can amount to hundreds, or even thousands, of pounds.

Then again, the majority of PMI policyholders are covered through group health insurance schemes provided by an employer (either theirs or their partner's). Therefore, this should be your first port of call when looking into this cover. Although you will be taxed on this 'benefit in kind' (perk), this is much cheaper than buying your own policy.

When shopping around for an individual policy, your yearly premium will vary based on your age, gender, occupation, smoking habits, medical history and state of health. Also, where you live and the level of cover you choose (basic, intermediate or advanced) will have a major impact on how much you pay.

One way to keep down the cost of private medical insurance is to buy a budget or 'cut down' policy. These only pay out if your treatment is not available on the NHS within a set period of time. Other policies bring down the cost by including a high policy excess, such as £2500 per year. This helps to cut down on the number and cost of claims, leading to significantly reduced premiums.

Although I view private medical insurance is a valuable perk for employees, I would think twice before buying it myself. The ongoing cost can be very high, which makes this insurance a luxury purchase. Then again, if you view private medical insurance as a necessity (for example, if you're self-employed), then it makes sense to shop around to get the biggest bang for your buck.

Start by checking financial-comparison website *www.moneysuper-market.com/medical*, then get quotes from leading providers *www.bupa.co.uk*, *www.axappphealthcare.co.uk* and *www.standard-lifehealthcare.co.uk*. Finally, use a specialist medical insurance broker such as *www.medibroker.co.uk* or another member of the Association of Medical Insurance Intermediaries at *www.amii.org.uk*.

Travel insurance (essential for holidaymakers and travellers)

In 2007, over 20 million British travellers took out travel insurance, which later led to more than 850,000 claims. Nevertheless, of the two million Brits who encounter trouble overseas each year, around 500,000 don't have any travel insurance. To me, this is an unfortunate mistake, as the right travel insurance policy can provide excellent coverage at a competitive price.

Many of the disasters that can happen abroad can be lessened by travel insurance. These problems include lost luggage, minor injuries, thefts, road traffic accidents and injury or illness. However, when choosing a policy, it's important to know the extent and limitations of your cover. Even more important is where you choose to buy your policy.

❝ never buy this cover from travel agents or tour operators ❞ The golden rule of travel insurance is: *never* buy this cover from travel agents or tour operators. Although this may be convenient, these providers usually charge inflated premiums for inferior policies. Indeed, some of these policies can be five to 10 times as expensive as Best Buy alternatives. Furthermore, buying from a travel firm will not give you the regulatory protection you get from using a registered broker or going direct to an insurance company. Until travel agents are regulated by the Financial Services Authority, they are not fit to sell travel insurance.

Rather than going to a single provider for travel insurance, it pays to conduct a wide search of the market. Whether you need a single-trip policy or an annual policy covering two or more overseas holidays, you should shop around for the best combination of cover versus price. This is particularly important if you plan to undertake any lively activities, such as skiing, snowboarding, bungee jumping, white-water rafting and other adventurous exploits.

For more advice on finding Best Buy travel insurance, visit *www.moneysavingexpert.com/insurance/cheap-travel-insurance*.

Six policies to shun

To round off this chapter, here are six types of insurance that I would urge you not to bother with:

■ *Boiler/central heating cover*: annual premiums of £200 add up to £2000 over 10 years. This would allow you to replace your boiler every six to eight years, so stick to putting an extra £15 a month into your emergency fund.

■ *Credit card protection plans*: As I warned in Chapter 2, these policies are overpriced and unnecessary. Why pay up to £25 a year for protection against financial fraud, when your legal liability is capped at just £50?

■ *Identity theft insurance*: instead of wasting £60 on this nonsense, buy a shredder to destroy personal financial documents and keep an eye on your credit record.

■ *Mobile phone insurance*: £120 a year to cover a handset costing £200? I'll rely on my contents insurance instead.

■ *Waiver of premium*: this is sickness insurance to cover monthly payments on a financial commitment, such as the premiums for an insurance policy. Insurance on insurance? No thanks!

■ *Wedding insurance*: if your big day is ruined because the chauffeur or photographer didn't turn up, will a payout really change things? Forget this insurance and spend the saving on a treat for your new spouse.

Three more tips on finding cheaper cover

- Be careful when you're given the choice of paying monthly, instead of yearly, premiums. Some insurance companies charge an annual interest rate of 25%+ for spreading your payments over a year!

- One simple way to reduce your premiums is to increase the voluntary excess payable in the event of a claim. This is a popular way to bring down the cost of car and home insurance.

- Likewise, improving your health and lifestyle habits will reduce the cost of life and health insurance policies. The biggest gain comes from giving up smoking.

Be honest – or lose out!

Insurance contracts are based on the principle of 'uberrimae fidei', a Latin phrase which means 'utmost good faith'. Thus, if you don't tell the truth to an insurance company, or omit crucial information, then there's little point in buying a policy at all.

Not being honest could lead to an insurer refusing to pay out when you claim, using 'non-disclosure' as its excuse. So, be sure to answer an insurer's questions fully and honestly, so that your insurance policy doesn't let you down. Otherwise, you're just throwing money down the drain.

Complaining about insurance policies

All life insurance, and almost all general (non-life) insurance policies, are regulated by the City watchdog, the Financial Services Authority (FSA). The FSA is responsible for ensuring that insurance companies treat customers fairly and adhere to its Insurance Code of Business.

If you have a problem with any of these policies (except travel insurance sold by travel firms and extended warranties sold by retailers), then your first step is to complain in writing to your insurer. If this fails to resolve your complaint, then take your case to the Financial Ombudsman Service.

Reclaiming rip-off premiums

After more than two decades in financial services, one thing is clear to me: the public is fed up with being ripped off by high-priced, low-value insurance policies. However, the tide is turning, largely thanks to consumer-champion websites such as *www.moneysavingexpert.com* and *www.fool.co.uk*.

❝ there is now a growing consumer campaign to reclaim rip-off premiums on mis-sold policies ❞

Indeed, there is now a growing consumer campaign to reclaim rip-off premiums on mis-sold policies. In particular, payment protection insurance is under attack as consumers learn how awful and overpriced this cover is. For more information on fighting back, visit *www.moneysavingexpert.com/ reclaim/ppi-loan-insurance*.

6

Turning into an intelligent investor

I n this chapter, we look at how to invest over the long term in order to build wealth. Although investing is perceived as a complex and challenging field, it could be argued that the basics of investing are, in fact, fairly straightforward. What's more, long-term investing is a sure-fire way to enrich yourself, as I've discovered in more than two decades as a private investor.

What is investing?

It is important to understand the big difference between saving and investing. Saving involves depositing money in a savings account with a bank or building society in order to earn interest on your spare cash. This is a low-risk activity, because deposit accounts are seen as being fairly safe and secure pots.

On the other hand, investing in assets other than cash involves taking greater risks than saving, but tends to produce higher returns in the long run. Indeed, at times, investing resembles a roller-coaster ride as asset prices move up and down seemingly at random. Hence, timing your entry into, and exit from, an investment is a very difficult game. This is why it makes sense to smooth out the ups and downs by investing over long periods – decades, even.

In essence, investing depends on three variables: how much money you can afford to set aside, how long you can leave it, and the size of the returns you make in the intervening period. Hence, you can create a better outcome by investing more, being patient and making higher investment returns while you do so.

Saving versus investing: the fall of Northern Rock

A classic example of the sharp contrast in the risks between saving and investing can be summed up by the experiences of Northern Rock savers and shareholders. When this building-society-turned-bank got into difficulty in September 2007, savers rushed to withdraw their cash. The government, frantic about the first run on a British bank for over 140 years, stepped in to guarantee 100% of savers' deposits.

On the other hand, Northern Rock's shareholders – its owners – saw the value of their investment plunge from a high of £12.58 per share in February 2007 to just 90p a year later. That's a top-to-bottom fall of almost 93% by the time Northern Rock was nationalised. What's more, it may well be the case that Northern Rock shares may later be judged nearly worthless, leaving its shareholders with next to nothing.

There are two ways to make money from investing

The first question to ask is: what's the point of investing? The answer is incredibly simple: turning cash into more cash further down the line. Essentially, there are two ways for your investments to generate cash (or its equivalent).

The first is through *capital gains* – making a profit by selling an asset, such as a share, for more than you paid for it. Often, this profit will be liable to capital gains tax (CGT). However, the well-known exception to this rule is when you sell your principal private residence (your main home). Thanks to steeply rising house prices between 1995 and 2007, British homeowners made trillions of pounds of tax-free profit simply from owning a home.

The second way to create cash from investments is through collecting the *income* generated from an asset. For a savings account, this income is the savings interest. For an investment property, the income comes from monthly rent payments. With shares, the income comes from the cash distributions paid to shareholders, usually half-yearly or quarterly, which are known as dividends.

Some investors look for capital growth, while others prefer to seek income. However, what you should be looking at is the *total return* – what you gain from the combination of both growth *and* income. So, although there is great debate between growth and income investors, the fact remains that the higher the total return, the more rewarding and attractive the investment, regardless of its 'label'. Indeed, experienced investors view growth and income as two sides of the same coin.

In which assets can you invest?

Other than cash, the four most popular assets in which to invest are:

- property (via buy-to-let or commercial property);
- shares (buying part-ownership of companies, large and small);
- bonds (IOUs issued by companies or governments);
- commodities (foodstuffs and livestock, base and precious metals, oil and energy).

A warning about 'alternative' investments

In addition to the five main asset classes mentioned above, there is a whole range of so-called 'alternative' investments, including antiques, art, books, cars, coins, gemstones, stamps, whisky and wine.

However, this book gives no advice on buying and selling alternative investments. Quite simply, investing outside of the mainstream requires a level of expertise which few of us could attain. Furthermore, there are several problems with investing in alternative asset classes, such as:

■ Unlike the main asset classes, alternative investments don't generate any income.

■ These items can be difficult to value, buy and sell.

■ There can be a lack of liquidity, making it difficult to buy and sell these items.

■ As these valuables are not traded on any recognised exchange, these markets are entirely unregulated. Thus, buyers enjoy none of the consumer protection available to financial investors.

■ Buying and selling commissions can be extremely high, especially at auction.

■ An expert guide is required to value goods and confirm their provenance (origin).

■ It can be incredibly hard to determine whether an item is genuine or fake. Hence, there have been numerous scams involving alternative investments.

In summary, it is extremely difficult to place a value on many of these assets. Thus, trying to predict their future worth is largely a speculative gamble. So, stick to investing in financial assets and leave alternative investments to the experts!

In my view, alternative investments should be viewed as a hobby or interest, that is, 'pleasure before treasure'. What's more, during economic booms, the price of fine art and so on tends to go through the roof. Thus, there's a danger that you could lose out by buying just as, say, the art market hits the peak of another cyclical boom.

How do you invest?

Quite simply, there are three routes you can choose when deciding how to invest:

1 *Do it yourself (DIY)*
   With the DIY route, you do without the advice of experts. Instead, you make your own investment decisions, pick your own shares, and so on. Thanks to strong growth in online

stock-broking and the emergence of a whole host of financial websites, DIY investing is becoming increasingly popular. However, this route can be challenging, as you have no one else to blame when you lose money!

2   *Hire someone to do it for you*
There is no shortage of investment experts willing to give you the benefit of their wisdom and experience. However, as you'd expect, this expertise comes at a price. You can look forward to parting with a yearly fee of up to 3% of your investment in return for this service.

Of course, these fees and other charges reduce the returns generated by underlying assets. Thus, over the long term, they gobble up a significant chunk of your capital. Furthermore, if your money manager doesn't perform up to scratch, paying high fees for inferior returns can be very frustrating!

3   *Let the market do the work for you*
If you don't understand (or can't be bothered to learn) the finer points of financial markets, then a simple, low-cost alternative is to get the markets themselves to work for you. Rather than seeking to beat a market by focusing on a tight group of assets or an accomplished fund manager, you simply invest in the entire market. You can do this through index trackers (see below) and similar market-following investments.

Where should you invest?

This is perhaps the biggest question in investment. Sadly, it is one that has no single answer. Indeed, your future success as an investor will depend largely on your 'asset allocation' – in which assets you choose to park your money.

For example, a portfolio heavily exposed to property would have performed very badly in the early Nineties. However, during the housing boom which began in the mid-Nineties, a portfolio concentrated in property would have produced bumper returns.

Likewise, a heavy weighting in shares would have been great in the 'bull' (rising) market of the late Nineties, but would have recorded disappointing results since the turn of the century. Indeed, at times when the economy is shaky and asset prices are falling across the board, it is said that only 'cash is king'.

Often, seasoned investment professionals construct 'model portfolios' aimed at giving balanced exposure to a broad range of assets, such as bonds, cash, commodities, property and shares. For example, one split might be, say, a tenth (10%) in commodities, a fifth (20%) in bonds and cash, three-tenths (30%) in property and the remainder (40%) in shares.

❝ one thing is for certain: the future is uncertain ❞

By dividing your capital among a range of assets, you help to diversify (spread) your risk and, therefore, reduce your exposure to any market. Thus, when prices start to tumble in one area, you do not lose out excessively. However, although one model for asset allocation may have worked well in the past, there is no guarantee that it will do so in the future. One thing is for certain: the future is uncertain!

Hence, asset allocation is really down to you and your own attitude towards risk. If you feel particularly comfortable allocating more money to a particular asset class, then by all means do so. For example, you may find property investing easier to understand than picking shares in the stock market. Then again, always remember that 'past performance is no guide to the future' and that your judgement may well prove to be faulty. The best investors recognise, and take account of, their own failings and shortcomings.

This spreading of your money between asset classes is known as 'diversification'. However, diversifying can backfire if you go chasing after the latest fashionable investment. In other words, diversification always makes sense if you're buying assets cheaply. On the other hand, if you follow the 'hot money' into the latest fad, then it could become *diworseification*!

Finally, understand that putting all of your eggs in one basket ('concentrating your portfolio') can work wonders if you pick the right sector in which to invest. However, this can lead to savage losses in future downturns. Therefore, whatever you do, make sure that you don't 'bet the farm' on any single asset class or company. Otherwise, you could end up inflicting permanent damage on your wealth!

In the remainder of this chapter, we will concentrate on investing in shares. We have already looked at saving in cash in Chapter 4. Successful investing in commodities requires a degree of expertise and knowledge which would require an entire book to explain. Property investing is covered in great detail in dozens, if not hundreds, of books. Hence, I will only skate over these topics in this section.

A quick word about bonds

A bond is an IOU issued by a company, government or other organisation. By buying such an IOU, you lend money to a company and get two things in return. First, a yearly income fixed for the life of the bond and, second, repayment of the bond at a prearranged date in the future ('on maturity'). As the interest paid by bonds is fixed, they are known as 'fixed-income instruments'.

Bonds are usually listed by reference to three things: their issuer, 'coupon' (the interest rate) and repayment date. For example, a 'BP 6% 2020' bond tells you:

1   The bond issuer is oil giant BP.

2   The coupon, or annual interest rate on your original investment, is 6% a year.

3   The bond will be repaid in the year 2020.

As bonds pay a fixed rate of interest throughout their life, their value alters when prevailing interest rates change. Indeed, the value of a bond rises as interest rates fall, and vice versa. Think about it like this: although general interest rates have fallen, the payout from our bond remains the same. In other words, this bond income has become more valuable relative to other assets. Thus, the value of the bond rises to reflect this higher income. On the other hand, if interest rates rise, bond prices fall, because the value of their fixed income has reduced relative to other income-generating assets.

When you buy a bond, you are exposed to 'credit risk' – the possibility that the company will be unable to pay the coupon and, even worse, the company cannot repay this IOU at its maturity date. Thus, when a company gets into financial difficulty, the market responds by writing down (placing a lower value) on its bonds. Hence, bonds are given a credit rating based on their issuer's financial strength, ranging from AAA (the highest) to C (the lowest).

Bonds issued by governments, called 'sovereign debt', are usually more highly rated than those issued by companies. This is because governments, particularly those in the developed world, are unlikely to default on their debt. In the UK, government bonds are known as 'gilts'; in the USA, they are 'Treasurys'; in Germany, 'Bunds'.

One problem with bonds is that they are designed to generate income, rather than capital growth. Indeed, a bond held from issue (launch) through to maturity will normally be redeemed (paid back) at the same price, known as 'par'. Then again, it is possible to make capital gains – or losses – from buying and selling bonds during their life.

In summary, bonds issued by financially strong companies and governments can be seen as relatively safe havens. They are riskier than cash deposits, but this may be reflected through payment of a higher income. However, they are considerably less risky than shares, especially during economic downturns. You can buy corporate and government bonds through a stockbroker. In addition, you can buy gilts directly through the Post Office.

If you don't wish to buy individual bonds, then you can invest in a range of bonds by buying into a bond fund. This is managed by a professional fund manager who pools investors' money in order to buy a wide range of bonds. Depending on your appetite for risk, you can choose from bond funds which specialise in investment-grade bonds (with high credit ratings), high-yield (riskier) bonds, and bonds issued by overseas companies and emerging-market governments.

A quick word about property

As the 20th century moved into the 21st, share prices started to tumble. Indeed, during this 'bear market' of falling share prices, the FTSE 100 index fell sharply, tumbling by more than half (52%) between the end of 1999 and 12 March 2003, before staging a recovery. This steep decline left many investors shell-shocked and unwilling to commit more money to the stock market.

Over the same period, the UK housing market went from strength to strength. Indeed, in the five years from 2000 to 2005, the average price of a UK property almost doubled. Over this period, the Halifax House Price Index leapt from £86,095 to £170,043, a rise of 98%.

Naturally, this turn of events led many people to view their homes as a better investment than their pension funds and other financial assets. Thus, homeowners started to invest directly in property through buy-to-let investing. Indeed, more than a million people jumped on the buy-to-let bandwagon by becoming private landlords. Furthermore, other investors put their money into commercial property funds, as an alternative to buying individual properties.

Ideally, as a private landlord, you have two goals. First, generate sufficient rental income to meet your buy-to-let mortgage and other letting expenses. This income, expressed as a percentage of the purchase price, is known as the 'rental yield'. Second, you look forward to banking substantial capital gains from future appreciation (growth) in the value of a property.

Of course, you should not view becoming a private landlord as a licence to print money. Usually, it requires a great deal of hard work and ongoing investment. For example, you may have the hassle of dealing with awkward tenants, rent arrears and damage to your property. Likewise, you will need to put aside a sizeable amount for the maintenance and upkeep of your properties. Each year, you should aim to put between 1% and 1.5% of a property's value into a 'sinking fund' to pay for repairs, repainting every three years, and so on.

Thanks to gearing (borrowing money via a mortgage to invest alongside your deposit), the returns from property investing are magnified dramatically. In the good years, capital gains can be well into double digits (10%+ a year), or even three figures (100%+ returns on your underlying deposit).On the other hand, when property prices start to fall, these drops are also magnified. Large falls in property prices can lead to 'negative equity', where the value of a property is less than the loan secured on it.

For example, let's say that you buy a flat for £100,000, putting down a 10% deposit (£10,000) and borrowing the remainder. After a great year, house prices have risen by, say, a fifth and you have made £20,000. Although this is just 20% of the £100,000 purchase price, your equity has increased to £30,000 (£120,000 minus your mortgage of £90,000). In other words, thanks to the gearing provided by the home loan, you've tripled your original investment!

Now for the other side of the gearing coin: instead of a great year, you have a grim year, and the value of your flat *falls* by a fifth. You now have negative equity of £10,000 (£80,000 minus your mortgage of £90,000). In this scenario, your deposit has disappeared, plus you owe another 10 grand. Ouch!

Alas, after 12 years of rising house prices, some property investors have lost touch with the real risks of putting all their eggs in the property basket. With UK property prices falling sharply in 2008, and this weakness likely to persist for several years, now is not the ideal time to consider a significant investment in property. Hence, this book merely touches upon the basics of investing in bricks and mortar. However, if you are interested in pursuing the 'property millionaire' dream, then try reading *The Property Developer's Book of Checklists* by Sally Coulthard, Prentice Hall Life, 2009.

Investing in shares

The rest of this chapter is devoted to investing in businesses by buying their shares. Some people think of stock markets as the world's largest casinos, so investing in them is akin to gambling. However, this is a gamble with a crucial difference, because the odds are in *your* favour, not the casino's!

Buying into businesses is not like buying a lottery ticket

Strictly speaking, investing is neither gambling nor speculating. Indeed, as the celebrated US fund manager Peter Lynch once remarked, 'Although it's easy to forget sometimes, a share is not a lottery ticket ... it's part-ownership of a business.'

❝ your goal when investing in shares is to grab as big a slice as you can ❞

At its heart, investing isn't about making a quick buck, taking a risky punt, or hoping to double your money on an all-or-nothing bet. Your goal when investing in shares is to grab as big a slice as you can of the returns generated by British (and overseas) companies. By buying into successful, well-managed businesses, your money should grow and prosper over decades.

So, when you buy shares in a stock market-listed company, you become a part-owner in that business. Thus, if the business does well, you will benefit from capital gains and, usually, twice-yearly or quarterly dividends.

One way to boost your long-term returns is to reinvest these dividends by using them to buy yet more shares. This boosts your capital gains in the years to come, and research shows that reinvested dividends can account for up to half of your total returns in the long run. So, if you don't need your dividends today, then reinvest them in more shares to boost your returns tomorrow.

DIY investing: swotting up on individual shares

When a company is listed on the stock market, this means that, as a public company, its shares can be traded. In other words, ownership of the company can be transferred between investors who buy and sell its shares through a middleman known as a stockbroker. Obviously, the more shares you buy in a company, the higher the proportion of the company you own.

Is there one proven, guaranteed way to pick shares which will surely outperform the wider stock market over time? Of course there isn't (although high-yield investing – buying shares which pay generous dividends – comes pretty close). If there were, then we would all use this technique, none of us would beat the market (because we would *become* the market), and we'd all be back to square one. Therefore, if someone claims to have a fool-proof way of making money from shares, then they probably belong in Chapter 8 ('Steering clear of scams')!

One of the best ways to start looking at shares is to turn to the 'London Share Service' pages of the *Financial Times*. Here, you'll find information about thousands of companies listed on the London Stock Exchange and its junior market, AIM (the Alternative Investment Market).

For example, in the *Financial Times* of 12 July 2008, the very first share listed, in the Aerospace and Defence sector, is the global defence and aerospace company BAE Systems. Here's what's the FT listing tells you about this firm:

Company	Price	Change	2008 High	2008 Low	Yield	P/E	Volume ('000s)
BAE Sys	419.50	−12	514	410.25	3.1	14.3	11,172

■ The first piece of information tells you the **company name**, in this case, BAE Systems. Each listed company has an abbreviated 'EPIC code' used to identify its shares. For BAE, this code, or 'ticker' is BA.

- The **price** shown is the mid price (usually expressed in pence). This is the midpoint between the price at which you can sell BAE shares, known as the 'bid price' and the price at which you can buy these shares, known as the 'offer price'. The difference between the bid and offer prices is known as the 'spread'. For large companies, this spread can be tiny, even under 0.1%. However, for smaller companies, whose shares are less easy to trade (less 'liquid'), the spread can amount to 10% or more.

- The **change** shows the difference between yesterday's closing price and the previous day's. On Friday, 11 July 2008, BAE shares slipped 12p, or 2.8%. In volatile markets, it is not unusual for individual share prices to move up or down 5% or more in a single day.

- The **2008 High** shows the highest price reached by BAE shares in 2008. As you can see, the current share price is 94.5p below the peak of 514p. In other words, BAE shares are down almost a fifth (18.4%) from their high.

- Likewise, the **2008 Low** for BAE is 410.25p, just 9.25p below the current share price. Thus, BAE shares are trading at the low end of their 2008 valuation, just 2.3% above this low.

- The **yield** for BAE is 3.1%. In other words, the dividends paid out by the company over the course of the past year amount to 3.1% of the current share price. In other words, last year's dividends amounted to 13p. The dividend yield of a share can be likened to the interest rate on a savings account. However, unlike the savings interest, this rate is not guaranteed and dividends can rise, fall or be stopped if the company feels this is necessary.

- The **P/E**, or price-earnings ratio, is a measure of how expensive a share is, relative to the rest of the market. The P/E is obtained by dividing the current share price by the company's earnings (expressed in pence). A P/E of 14.3 means that it would cost 14.3p to buy 1p of BAE's annual earnings. On 11 July 2008, BAE's P/E was higher than that of the FTSE 100 index (10.45), of which it is a member.

■ Lastly, the **volume** shows the number of shares traded that day. In BAE's case, over 11 million shares changed hands in a single day. It is not unusual for millions, or tens of millions, of shares in the UK's biggest companies (known as 'blue chips') to be traded in one day. Conversely, trading in some small companies can be very low, even zero, on a day-to-day basis.

■ To find out the size of a listed company, multiply its share price by the number of shares in issue.

■ This figure, known as the 'market capitalisation', can amount to £100 billion for the biggest companies and under £1m for the smallest. Looking up BAE on the FT.com website, we find that it has 3525 million shares, so its 'market cap' on this date was £14,787 million. At almost £15 billion, BAE is one of the biggest firms listed on the London Stock Exchange.

Don't be fooled by the numbers!

So, given that we're looking for shares which make us money through dividends and capital gains, all we need to do is find cheap shares (those with low P/E ratios) with high dividend yields, correct? Alas, if only stock-picking were as easy as this!

Some companies have low P/E ratios for a good reason – perhaps they are growing very slowly, if at all. Indeed, they may have a low P/E because their earnings are about to slump, or they are on the brink of going out of business. Conversely, some high-growth and sought-after firms enjoy much higher P/E ratios relative to the wider market. So, in itself, the P/E ratio tells you very little about the relative attractiveness of a company and its shares.

Likewise, some companies appear to have high dividend yields because their share price has tumbled. For example, if a company's share price halved, this would double its dividend yield. However, if the company is struggling then it may decide to conserve cash by cutting the dividend, thus reducing the yield in future years. So, once again, a high dividend yield in itself is not a sure-fire way of picking shares.

In fact, the only way to decide whether a company is worth investing in is to trawl through the information provided by the company to its shareholders. Only by learning to read a firm's report and accounts, and by interpreting the complex financial information within, can you hope to reach a verdict on the attractiveness of a listed business.

As you've probably guessed by now, this book will not teach you investment strategies to pick shares. I'd be a charlatan if I claimed that I had an investment strategy to beat the market which worked for every investor. Nevertheless, if you fancy trying to make money by investing in individual firms, then try reading *How the Stock Market Really Works* by Leo Gough, published by FT Prentice Hall (Price: £19.99; ISBN: 978-0-273-71428-6).

Likewise, the award-winning Motley Fool website at *www.fool.co.uk* provides excellent advice and support for both new and experienced investors. For the record, I like this website so much that I joined it in 2003 and have written for it ever since. In addition, the *www.FT.com* website provides a wealth of information for investors new and old.

Harnessing the power of compound interest

Most investors agree that investing in shares is a long-term strategy. Arguably, the longer you invest, the greater your chance of success. Thus, when it comes to investing, your time in the market is usually more important than your timing of the market (choosing when to invest). Indeed, it's been said that the stock market is a vehicle for transferring wealth from impatient to patient investors!

This idea is best illustrated through a demonstration of the power of compound interest. If you leave your investments alone, and do not withdraw any dividends nor sell any shares, then the returns earned will 'compound up' over time. Here's an explanation of how this works:

Let's assume that your cash in a savings account earns 2% a year above the rate of inflation (the general rate at which prices rise).

The value of £100 growing at 2% or 5% a year

Years	Cash 2%	Shares 5%
1	102.00	105.00
2	104.04	110.25
3	106.12	115.76
4	108.24	121.55
5	110.41	127.63
10	121.90	162.89
20	148.59	265.33
30	181.14	432.19
40	220.80	704.00

*Note that this table shows assumed 'real' returns, after accounting for inflation.

Thus, £100 growing at 2% a year will be worth £102 after one year. After two years, it will be worth £104.04 – another £2 of interest, plus 4p of interest on the previous £2. After five years, your £100 will have grown to £110.41 and, after 40 years, it will have more than doubled to £220.80.

Now look at column three, which shows how your money might grow were it to be invested in shares which, over time, produced an average yearly return of 5% above inflation. After one year, your £100 is worth £105. After two years, it grows to £110.25; after five years, £127.63. After 40 years, it will have grown to an impressive £704, or more than seven times your original stake. Although these annual returns are not predictions of results to come, it is possible that they could be achieved in future.

In a nutshell, the superior growth generated by shares over the long term, together with the power of compound interest, explains why it makes sense to invest in the stock market. Quite simply, although you will experience ups and downs, and even periods of extreme turbulence akin to riding a roller-coaster, these will be mere blips in the long run. This explains why major investors such as pension funds and insurance companies keep the lion's share of their assets in shares, rather than in cash or other assets.

Monthly saving versus investing lump sums

One question investors often ask is: should I lump my money into the stock market all in one go, or should I drip-feed it in over a period of time? Once again, there is no definitive answer. Given that the rises and falls in the stock market are almost like a random walk, it's impossible to say when the most favourable time to invest is.

Nevertheless, some investors are convinced of the merits of 'pound-cost averaging'. This involves investing every month in order to take advantage of the fluctuations in share prices. However, given that share prices tend to rise over time, the counter argument is that you should put your money into the market as early as possible.

Of course, most investment beginners don't have a lump sum available to lob into the market. These people have no option but to 'drip feed' or 'phase in' their investment via monthly savings plans. Some may be tempted to 'time the market' by waiting for share prices to fall before adding their next sum. However, this is notoriously difficult to do, so I suggest playing it safe by investing when your bank balance is strongest (usually on payday).

Thus, my personal view is that you should invest whenever you have money to spare. However, if you have a large sum to invest and feel uneasy about whacking it into the market all in one go, then feel free to split it up into smaller sums and invest it over a period of months.

Choosing a stockbroker

When it comes to choosing a stockbroker, you have two choices. First, you can opt for a full-service stockbroker, who will make investment decisions on your behalf and charge you a pretty penny for doing so. Second, you can opt for a no-frills, usually online, execution-only (no advice) service which charges low fees for buying and selling shares and other stock market investments.

Personally, I've yet to be convinced of the merits of using a full-service 'advisory' stockbroker. There is no evidence that individuals employed by these firms can, and do, produce market-beating results in return for their steep fees. Hence, my preference is to use a low-cost online stockbroker. This means that I don't have paper share certificates. Instead, my shareholdings are held electronically in a nominee account which my broker administers on behalf of investors.

For more information on choosing a stockbroker, read the 10 tips at www.fool.co.uk/brokers/information/choosing-a-broker.aspx and try the share-dealing search engine at www.moneysupermarket.com/shares.

Employee share schemes (Sharesave/SAYE and Share Incentive Plans)

If you work for a listed company then your employer may give you the option to buy shares in it. By doing so, you can tip the odds of success in your favour, and also save tax on any profits you make. The two most popular employee share schemes are Sharesave and Share Incentive Plans.

Sharesave

Sharesave (alias, Save As You Earn) allows employees to save between £5 and £250 a month via payroll deduction for three or five years. It gives employees the right, but not the obligation, to buy shares at a future date, at a price determined just prior to this option being granted. The sponsoring company can discount this option price by up to a fifth (20%) off the market price at that time.

When your Sharesave scheme matures, you can use this cash, plus a tax-free bonus, to buy shares at the original discounted

> **simply take your savings and tax-free bonus and run**

price. If the market price is higher than your option price, then you've made a capital gain on your shares. The good news is that Sharesave comes with a built-in guarantee: if the market price has plunged below your option price during the life of your plan, you simply take your savings and tax-free bonus and run!

Around 2.3 million employees of listed companies save via Sharesave, making it one of the most popular employee incentives in the UK. Personally, I'm a huge fan, as both my wife and I have used Sharesave to build substantial wealth through relatively risk-free investing in our employers. For more information on Sharesave, read www.ifsproshare.org/help_&_ guidance/share_plan_fact_sheets/approved_plans/sharesave.cfm.

Share Incentive Plans (SIPs)

Share Incentive Plans (SIPs) were introduced in 2000. These SIPs fall into three categories:

1 Free shares: an employer can give free shares worth up to £3000 a year to employees. After a qualifying period of three to five years, these shares are free of income tax and National Insurance contributions.

2 Partnership shares: employees can buy shares from their before-tax salary, up to a limit of £125 a month or a tenth (10%) of salary, whichever is lower. Again, after a qualifying period of three to five years, these shares are free of income tax and NICs.

3 Matching shares: employers can give employees up to two free shares for each partnership share bought.

No capital gains tax is payable if shares are taken out of a SIP plan after five or more years.

So, SIPs give employees the opportunity to buy shares in their employer at a discount which, in effect, comes from savings on income tax and NICs. What's more, matching shares can produce even deeper markdowns: the most generous scheme ('buy one, get two free') can turn as little as £73.75 a month before tax into £375 on day one. That's an immediate gain of 408%!

For more information on share incentive plans, read *www.ifsproshare.org/help_&_guidance/share_plan_fact_sheets/approv ed_plans/sip.cfm*

Don't stake your future on your employer!

Although employee share schemes allow you to 'beat the market' by getting free or discounted shares, don't get too carried away. By investing heavily in your employer over many years, you could end up with one giant egg in your investment basket. If your employer then gets into difficulty, you could face the 'double trouble' of losing your job and a large slice of your wealth.

Therefore, if you have a large stash of shares in your employer, then do take steps to sell some shares every now and then, in order to diversify your holdings. Otherwise, you could lose out when your company's performance and share price take a turn for the worse.

For example, employees who bought shares in failed ex-FTSE 100 firms Marconi and Railtrack lost millions of pounds when these companies crashed. More recently, workers at leading investment bank Lehman Brothers were all but wiped out when the US government allowed it to fail. So, no matter how highly you rate your employer, don't put everything you have into it. After all, every company disappoints its investors at *some* point in time!

Save tax by sheltering investments inside Individual Savings Accounts (ISAs)

As I mentioned at the beginning of this chapter, your goal as an investor is to capture is much of the returns generated by companies as you possibly can. Earlier, I warned that high management charges can eat into your investment returns. Likewise, taxes on dividends and capital gains can also have a punishing effect on the long-term rewards of investing in shares.

Hence, the simple answer is to invest inside a tax shelter which helps to keep HM Revenue & Customs at bay. The most popular tax shelter in the UK is the Individual Savings Account, or ISA.

ISAs replaced two previous tax shelters, Personal Equity Plans (PEPs) and Tax Exempt Special Savings Accounts (TESSAs), in April 1999. Today, more than 17 million savers and investors dodge tax by putting cash into, or buying assets inside, ISAs. By 2007, £208 billion had been poured into ISAs in just eight years, making them the UK's favourite legal tax dodge.

I explained how to save inside cash ISAs in Chapter 4. However, you can also use ISAs to shelter shares, bonds and investment funds safe from tax. All capital gains made inside ISAs are tax free, so there is no capital gains tax at 18% to pay. Furthermore, higher-rate taxpayers can avoid paying any extra tax on dividends by holding shares inside ISAs.

In the 2008/09 tax year, the following ISA contribution limits apply:

ISA type	Limit (£)
Cash	3600
Shares	7200

Note that you cannot contribute the maximum amount to both types of ISA. For example, if you pay £100 into a cash ISA, then the most you can pay into a shares ISA falls to £7100. Also, if you put the maximum £3600 into a cash ISA, then you can still put up to £3600 into a shares ISA.

So, make sure that you make full use of your ISA allowance. Otherwise, you could end up paying tax needlessly. For more information on ISAs, visit www.fool.co.uk/isas.

Index trackers – letting the market do the work

Although there is no perfect strategy to maximise the return from investing in shares, letting the stock market do the work for you comes a close second.

As I explained earlier, most adults lack the time, skill and experience needed to manage their own investments. On the other hand, employing the services of investment professionals is expensive and is no guarantee of success. Thanks to their high charges, most 'actively managed' stock-picking funds fail to beat the stock market over long periods.

For the record, it's estimated that at least four out of five fund managers – *more than 80%* – produce inferior returns for their investors over 20 years or more. In fact, it could be argued that the majority of investment funds are run for the benefit of their managers, rather than their owners. When it comes to getting rich, the annual management charge could equally be called the annual *Maserati* charge!

Because of the high ongoing cost of employing expensive stock-pickers, I believe that, on average, most investors would be better off putting their money into the cheapest, simplest stock market vehicle: an index-tracking fund, or 'index tracker'.

An index tracker does what it says on the tin: it passively tracks a particular stock market index up and down, without any human decision-making. Thanks to their ultra-low charges, index trackers invest a higher proportion of investors' money into the stock market. Thus, this head start gives investors in index trackers both a short-term and long-term advantage. (There are also index trackers to track other markets, such as bonds, commodities and property.)

The big problem with an index tracker is that, by definition, it cannot beat the wider market. Indeed, thanks to its modest charges, it is destined slightly to underperform its index each year. Furthermore, slight deviations from the index, known as tracking errors, do occur.

Another drawback with index trackers is that some trackers are better at tracking a particular index than others. This is because it is just about impossible to track an index perfectly. To do so, you'd have to buy each company in an index in exactly the right proportion, which is unbelievably difficult.

Thus, many trackers buy into the major constituents of an index (the really big firms) and then 'synthesise' their exposure to the remaining firms via complex financial instruments known as derivatives. Hence, before investing in a tracker, ask its manager for its 'tracking error' or 'tracking deviation'. If this turns out to be sizeable (say, more than 0.5% a year), then ask for an explanation for this deviation.

Of course, like their actively managed rivals, index trackers pay dividends to their owners. In addition, you can shelter an index tracker inside a tax-free ISA wrapper.

When compared with the rest of investing theory, choosing a tracker is child's play. All you do is choose the lowest-charging fund which tracks a particular index. For example, investing in a FTSE All-Share index tracker gives you exposure to around 700 of the UK's largest listed firms. Since many of these are global businesses, you also get exposure to the wider global economy.

At the date of writing, the cheapest FTSE All-Share index tracker was the Fidelity Moneybuilder UK Index fund, which has a total expense ratio of 0.27% a year. Indeed, this fund has the lowest charges of any widely available investment fund in the UK.

Which index you choose to track is up to you. Personally, I prefer to throw my net as wide as I can, in order to capture the returns from as wide a range of businesses as possible. Therefore, I prefer FTSE All-Share trackers to FTSE 100 (the giants) and FTSE 250 (mid-sized firms) trackers. Also, as you become more experienced at investing, you can branch out by investing in foreign trackers. There are index trackers covering every major stock market in the world, including those in the US, Europe, Japan and emerging markets (developing countries).

You can find a list of index-tracking funds at *www.trustnet.com/ut/funds/perf.aspx?sec=ind* (54 were listed in July 2008). Also, you can search for low-charging funds at *www.fsa.gov.uk/tables/bespoke/UnitTrust*.

Exchange Traded Funds (ETFs) – a popular alternative to index trackers

Exchange Traded Funds (ETFs) behave like index-tracking funds, but can be bought and sold in the same way as shares. ETFs were first launched in the UK in 2000. Eight years later, there were more than 140 different ETFs from which to choose.

As well as ETFs which track the world's major stock markets, there are those which track bonds, commodities and other investments. The market leader for EFTs in the UK is iShares, a division of Barclays Global Investors, which you can find at *www.ishares.co.uk*.

As ETFs have become more popular and have grown in size, their costs have come down and have helped to reduce charges on rival index-tracking funds. As ETFs are bought through stockbrokers, you have to pay dealing charges when you buy or sell them. However, unlike buying shares directly, you don't have to pay stamp duty of 0.5% when you buy ETFs, giving them a further edge.

In summary, for cheap and flexible investment in stock and other markets, ETFs are hard to beat. For more information on ETFs, visit *www.trustnet.com/help/etf*.

Unit trusts and open-ended investment companies (OEICs)

The majority of UK investors invest via collective investments – funds where investors' money is pooled together by a fund manager, who then buys and sells shares on their behalf. The vast majority of these funds are actively managed, which means that the fund manager and his/her research team pursue their own investment strategy.

Most investors in collective funds put their money into two particular types of funds, known as unit trusts (UTs) and open-ended investment companies (OEICs, pronounced 'oiks'). In July 2008, fund website *www.trustnet.com* listed 2346 different UTs and OEICs!

UTs and OEICs are called open-ended funds, because they do not have a fixed size. In other words, the fund increases in size when investors put in money, and it shrinks when investors withdraw their cash. In most cases, you can deposit lump sums or save monthly into both UTs and OEICs.

You do this by purchasing units in a unit trust or OEIC, either directly from the fund manager, or via a financial adviser or other intermediary. The cheapest way to do so is via a fund supermarket or discount broker (see below). Unlike shares, whose prices move about throughout trading days, the prices for unit trusts and OEICs are calculated once a day, usually at noon. You buy units in a unit trust or OEIC when the price is next set, which is often the next day.

With unit trusts, there are two prices, the bid price at which you can sell units, and the offer price at which you buy units. The difference ('spread') between these two prices makes up the initial charge for investing in unit trusts. In many cases, this initial charge can be up to 6% upfront, but this can be dramatically reduced by discount brokers. OEICs have only one price, with any initial charge being collected separately.

As well as charging initial fees, unit trusts and OEICs charge ongoing annual management charges (AMCs). These can exceed 2% a year, but a number of low-cost funds charge 1% or less. Furthermore, other charges, including administration, audit and trustee fees can bump up a fund's total expense ratio (TER) to as much as 3% a year. Lastly, some unit trusts and OEICs also levy exit fees when you remove your money.

So, before you invest in a unit trust, OEIC or other investment fund, take a long, hard look at its initial charge and total expense ratio. Over a 10-year period, these charges could easily swallow up a third of your entire investment. As I said earlier, many investment funds enrich their managers far more than they do their owners!

Fund supermarkets and discount brokers

One way to reduce the high upfront and ongoing charges associated with investment funds is to avoid investing directly with a fund manager. Instead, you can invest cheaply by employing the services of a low-cost discount broker or fund supermarket. Just as online stockbrokers allow you to buy shares cheaply, these firms enable you to eliminate upfront charges and obtain lower ongoing fees.

In order to provide this 'pile it high, sell it cheap' service, most discount brokers and fund supermarkets operate exclusively online. The most popular of these services include:

Best Invest	*www.bestinvest.co.uk*
Cavendish Online	*www.cavendishonline.co.uk*
Chartwell	*www.chartwell-investment.co.uk*
Chelsea Financial Services	*www.chelseafs.co.uk*
Fidelity's FundsNetwork	*www.fundsnetwork.co.uk*
Hargreaves Lansdown	*www.h-l.co.uk*
Torquil Clark	*www.tqonline.co.uk*

From personal experience, I would recommend Hargreaves Lansdown and Cavendish Online for their range of discounts on offer and superior customer service.

Guaranteed equity bonds

One thing that investors are desperate to do is avoid the impact of falling share prices. This has led to substantial growth in 'structured finance' products known as Guaranteed Equity Bonds (GEBs). In essence, GEBs are a halfway house between the safety of cash deposits and the risky – but superior – returns offered by the stock market. Unlike corporate and government bonds, GEBs do not pay any income. Instead, they pay out a return on maturity based on stock-market performance.

By investing a lump sum in a GEB, you tie up your money for a fixed period, usually five years. Hence, early withdrawals will trigger exit penalties, reducing the amount which you get back. On maturity, the payout from a GEB is based on the performance of one or more stock market indices. If the market has risen then you receive a fixed return, say, 110% of the rise in the index. If the market has fallen then you usually get your money back in full and, in some cases, a small fixed percentage return.

The first problem with GEBs is that they come with inbuilt charges which can gobble up to 7% of your lump sum, of which around 3% will be paid to your financial adviser in commission. However, you won't notice these charges, because they are hidden away within the structure of the bond.

The second problem is that GEBs don't pay any interest or dividends. In mid-July 2008, the yield on the FTSE All-Share index was 4.38%. In other words, by investing in a GEB linked to the FTSE All-Share, you give up dividends worth almost 4.4% a year. Over five years, this compounds up to almost a quarter (24%) of your money. It is this loss that covers the cost of your no-lose guarantee, plus the GEB provider's charges and profits.

In my view, GEBs offer the worst of both worlds. When stock markets are rising, GEBs produce inferior returns than you would earn from investing directly in the stock market. What's more, in falling markets, your loss is reduced by the dividend income paid by shares. In addition, you pay a hefty premium for a GEB's no-lose promise. History suggests that the UK stock market rarely falls over any five-year period – about one time in 20, in fact. So, who really needs this guarantee at all?

** these companies aim to make tidy profits from investors' ignorance **

Furthermore, Guaranteed Equity Bonds have been heavily promoted by various high street banks, building societies and other financial organisations. This should be a warning sign in itself, as these companies aim to make tidy profits from investors' ignorance. In short, GEBs are complicated and expensive, and are best avoided!

Enterprise Investment Schemes (EISs) and Venture Capital Trusts (VCTs)

As we near the end of this chapter, I think it's worth mentioning two tax havens used by experienced and wealthier investors.

Venture Capital Trusts (VCTs)

A Venture Capital trust is an investment company which buys stakes in start-up businesses and small companies. Like shares, these trusts are quoted on the London Stock Exchange. As you'd imagine, failure rates among small firms can be high, so VCTs can be considered high-risk investments and only suitable for experienced investors.

The attraction of VCTs is the tax incentives on offer. A £1000 investment into a VCT qualifies for an upfront income tax rebate of 30% (£300), provided the shares are held for at least five years. What's more, all capital gains and dividends from VCTs are tax free, subject to a three-year holding period.

You can invest up to £200,000 each tax year into VCTs, but you can only reclaim as much tax as you've paid in that year. However, this tax relief is only available if you invest in a VCT when it launches or offers investors new shares. It is not paid to investors who buy 'second-hand' VCT shares on the stock market.

As you'd expect, VCT managers take hefty fees from your investment. Typically, initial charges are around 5%, and annual charges about 3%. In addition, VCT managers often take performance fees and other incentives, which further reduce investors' returns. Another problem is that, once listed, VCT shares are illiquid (difficult to trade) and bid-offer spreads can be enormous, often exceeding 30%.

In summary, investing in VCTs should be left to wealthy, long-term investors. Don't let the generous tax breaks on offer blind you to the drawback of investing in these complex investments. In stock market speak, 'don't let the tax tail wag the investment dog'!

Enterprise Investment Schemes (EISs)

With an EIS, you invest directly in a single (often unquoted) trading company which has to satisfy certain criteria regarding its size (it must have gross assets of under £7 million immediately prior to investment) and the trade it conducts. After holding onto EIS shares for three years, you receive four tax benefits:

1   20% income-tax relief on up to £500,000 per tax year invested in new shares.

2   No capital gains tax (CGT) on any gains made on qualifying shares.

3   Loss relief against income or capital gains for losses made when you dispose of qualifying EIS shares after three years.

4   Unlimited CGT deferral. CGT can be deferred if an EIS investment is made within one year before or three years after the sale which produced the capital gain to be deferred.

However, the dividends paid by EIS shares are not tax free. This example shows how EIS tax reliefs work:

EIS share investment of £10,000
Deduct 20% income tax relief of £2000
Deduct 18% CGT deferral of £1800
Thus, the net cost of EIS investment is £6200

In effect, the taxman gives EIS investors an interest-free loan of the CGT, which is repaid later when the EIS shares are sold.

Again, EISs are complex, highly illiquid and potentially risky investments which are suitable only for wealthy, experienced, long-term investors. Don't invest in an EIS without taking proper professional advice. For more information on both VCTs and

EISs, consult a specialist financial adviser, such as Allenbridge Group at *www.taxshelterreport.co.uk*.

Find your own investing style

As I have repeated several times in this chapter, it's up to you to find the investing style which works best for you. You may prefer the simple approach of harnessing the stock market through index-tracking funds. Alternatively, you may prefer to leave the investment decisions to a fund manager, while making sure that you don't overpay for this service. Then again, you may decide to take your own investment decisions, perhaps by becoming a high-yield or value investor searching for cheap shares.

As the old saying goes, the choice is yours. Don't be afraid to change your investing strategy if you feel that it is not meeting your goals and attitude to risk. At the end of the day, no-one is forcing you to pursue one investing strategy over another. Don't be bullied or cajoled into pursuing an investment strategy which doesn't suit your long-term financial objectives!

66 the choice is yours 55

My final word

If you're keen to lose a lot of money, then try chasing the 'hot money' by following the latest investment fashion. For example, during the dotcom boom around the turn of the century, investors rushed to pour money into high-tech Internet, media and telecoms firms. Naturally, technology funds were set up in order to grab a slice of this wave of money.

As always happens, this 'new paradigm' proved to be a mirage, and many of these miracle businesses went bust before ever making a profit. Likewise, the performance of the hyped-up technology funds suffered terribly, with many losing more than nine-tenths (90%+) of investors' money. So, don't be a nerd and follow the herd, because today's star fund often turns into tomorrow's dog!

Finally, if you find yourself disappointed at the content of this chapter, then I've done my job properly. My goal is to show you that there is no 'magic spell' for making money from investing. So, please view this introduction to investing as bait, rather than a banquet. Your job now is to turn disappointment into delight by doing your own research, reading more about investing, and perhaps having a stab at it yourself. When it comes to investing, particularly in the stock market, there is no substitute for personal experience!

Pumping up your pension

I n this chapter, we learn one of the key financial lessons in life: how to fund the shift from work to retirement. During working life, most of our income is earned, either from employment or self-employment. During retirement, most of our income is unearned, and is made up of the income paid by pensions and the returns generated by other assets.

Retirement and the need for unearned income

In many ways, retirement is like the beginning of a completely new life. After all, if you have spent most of your adult years in full-time work, then the transition from employment to retirement can be difficult. Of course, retirement does not necessarily mean stopping work permanently. You may decide to continue working part-time in order to supplement your income and cut down on your free time. Alternatively, you could do some paid consultancy work, or unpaid voluntary work for a good cause which is close to your heart.

66 your goal is to enjoy your later years to their fullest 55

Thanks to increased life expectancy, most adults can expect to live well into their seventies, eighties and even beyond. For many, life after work is all about spending their time productively while living within modest means. Thus, in some ways, it's a good idea to regard retirement as one long holiday. Your goal is to enjoy your later years to their fullest, while making sure that you don't run out of money during the trip!

Retirement is often a long game

When it comes to providing for a prosperous retirement, you can ask these three groups for help:

1 the government (through state pensions);

2 your employer (through occupational pensions); and

3 yourself (through personal/private pensions and other investments).

Of course, the person with your best interests at heart is the only one you can really trust to safeguard your future: yourself. Furthermore, thanks to increases in life expectancy and falling investment returns, the cost of providing pensions has soared over the past decade. Therefore, anyone relying on the continued generosity of the government and British businesses could be in for a nasty shock at retirement!

The big problem with pension provision is that, thanks to improved nutrition and medical care, people are living far longer than they did 50 years ago. It used to be the case that a man retiring at 65 might only claim his pensions for perhaps five years before dying. These days, someone retiring at 65 might easily live another 15 years, placing far greater stress on pension schemes, both public and private.

Of course, as with all things in life, the key to a rewarding retirement is to be positive and plan ahead. To maximise your chances of having a comfortable retirement, your retirement planning should begin in early adulthood and continue throughout your working life. Indeed, the ideal situation would be to contribute to a pension from the very beginning to the very end of your career. After all, financing 20 years of retirement requires huge reserves.

What is a pension?

It is possible to save for retirement using various different assets and savings vehicles, including pensions, savings, shares and property. However, most retirement planning is centred on pensions. Quite simply, a pension is a specialised investment vehicle designed to provide an income to workers when they retire.

Of course, the government is very keen to encourage workers to take steps to fund their retirement. Hence, it provides highly attractive tax breaks to pensions, in order to promote their take-up amongst workers. Indeed, the tax incentives given to contributions make pensions among the most tax-advantaged products available. Thus, although pensions are far from perfect, their tax-favoured status gives them a head start over other methods of saving for retirement.

The new era for pensions

Prior to 6 April 2006, known as 'pensions A-Day', there were many different sets of rules and regulations governing pensions. However, nowadays there is a single, simpler rule book governing both personal and occupational pensions.

Today, almost all adults can save as much as they like to any number and type of pension plans. Furthermore, you can receive tax relief – extra money from HM Revenue & Customs – on contributions of up to 100% of your yearly earnings until the age of 75. Then again, there is a maximum annual allowance that you can pay into a pension each year while still receiving tax relief. Nevertheless, at £235,000 in the 2008/09 tax year, this has no practical impact on 99.9% of adults.

In addition, there is a further restriction governing the combined value of your pension pots. In the 2008/09 tax year, this lifetime allowance is £1.65 million, rising to £1.8 million by 2010/11. Amounts in excess of this threshold will be taxed at up to 55%, although some protection can be claimed for pensions in force before April 2006. Again, given the large sums involved, this is unlikely to worry the vast majority of workers.

Tax relief: the 'bait' for pensions

The regulatory framework and tax treatment of pensions has evolved over many decades. Although this has made pensions relatively inflexible (see 'The pitfalls of pensions' below), it has turned them into an attractive tax shelter. The biggest incentive for paying into a pension is that you receive tax relief on your contributions. In effect, this tax relief gives you back the tax which you've already paid on your earnings.

Four in five workers pay the basic rate of income tax, which is 20% in 2008/09. Thus, after basic-rate tax, £100 of pay is reduced to £80. However, if this £80 is paid into a pension, then HMRC automatically gives back the £20 tax paid in the form of pension tax relief. Thus, every 80p paid into a pension attracts a rebate of 20p, boosting contributions by a quarter (25%).

Higher-rate taxpayers, who pay income tax at 40%, can claim a further 20% tax rebate from HMRC. You can do this via your yearly SA100 (tax return), or by writing to your local inspector of taxes. Note that it's up to you to claim this extra relief, as your employer may not automatically do this for you.

So, to summarise: a pension contribution of £100 costs a basic-rate taxpayer £80 after tax relief. For higher-rate taxpayers, the net contribution (after claiming extra relief) is a mere £60.

" anyone (including children) can contribute "

What about people who don't pay tax or don't have any earnings? The good news is that anyone (including children) can contribute up to £3600 each tax year into a stakeholder or personal pension and still collect basic-rate tax relief. So, even though they have paid no income tax, they still get the 25% uplift from tax relief. Thus, a £3600 contribution would break down into a 'net' payment of £2880 plus £720 of tax relief (20% of £3600).

A pile of different pensions

During the course of your working life, you are likely to build up pensions from various different sources: your own pension plans, work-based schemes, and state pensions.

State pensions

As well as pensions built up in your own funds and by your employers, you will also receive pension income from the state at the end of your working life

Basic state pension

When you reach your normal state pension age, the government's Pension Service will begin paying your state pension. At present, state pension age is 60 for women and 65 for men. However, the cost of supporting a rapidly ageing population is placing a strain on the government's finances. Therefore, between 2010 and 2020, the state pension age for women will gradually increase to 65. Between 2024 and 2028, the state pension age for both men and women will increase to age 68.

In order to claim your state pension, you should contact the Department for Work and Pensions (DWP) three months before you reach state retirement age. By requesting and completing a BR1 claim form, you can be sure of getting your state pension as soon as you are entitled to receive it.

How much you receive from the state will depend on your National Insurance Contribution (NIC) record. At present, the full basic state pension is paid to men who have paid (or been credited with) NICs for 44 years. For women, 39 years of NICs will secure the full state pension. Then again, people retiring after 5 April 2010 will only need 30 years of NICs to obtain the full state pension. Thus, for women retiring before 6 April 2010, it may be worthwhile plugging the gaps in their NIC record by paying extra 'buy back' contributions.

Of course, the lower your number of years of NICs, the lower your state pension will be. This is a particular problem for women, since their working life is often interrupted by caring for children or elderly relatives. However, married women aged over 60 who do not have enough qualifying years based on their own NICs can get a state pension based on their husband's NICs.

Likewise, widows and widowers may be entitled to a basic state pension based on their late spouse's NIC record. Furthermore, women on maternity leave or carers' leave can fill in the gaps in their NIC record during their working life by applying for a benefit known as 'home responsibilities protection'.

Although we cannot say how much the state pension will be worth in future years, it's fair to argue that its value will continue to decline relative to overall earnings. For the record, in the 2008/09 tax year, the basic state pension for a single person is £90.70 a week, which is just over £4716 a year. Pensioners aged 80 or over receive an 'age addition', worth a princely 25p a week. As you can see, the state pension is hardly generous and will not support even a subsistence-level lifestyle!

❝ the state pension is hardly generous ❞

Additional state pensions

As well as the basic state pension, employees are entitled to an additional state pension known as the State Second Pension (S2P). Self-employed workers are not entitled to the S2P, formerly known as SERPS (the State Earnings Related Pension Scheme). The amount you receive from the State Second Pension is based on your NIC record and your earnings during your career. Naturally, the higher your earnings and the longer you have paid NICs, the larger your S2P will be.

On the other hand, some workers have elected to opt out of the State Second Pension. Instead, they redirect some of their NICs into a company or personal pension. For every year that you remain contracted out from S2P or SERPS, you lose that year's entitlement to this additional pension. In its place, you build up an extra pension inside your company or private scheme.

The subject of state pensions and benefits is an absolute maze which gets more complicated every year. So, for further information on state pensions and other benefits, visit:

- Age Concern at *www.ageconcern.org.uk*
- Entitled To at *www.entitledto.co.uk*
- Help the Aged at *www.helptheaged.org.uk*
- The Department for Work and Pensions at *www.dwp.gov.uk*
- The Pension Service at *www.thepensionservice.gov.uk*

Pension Credit and means testing

There are around 11.4 million pensioners in the UK, who account for almost a quarter (24%) of voters. Of course, governments don't want to upset this powerful lobby, so they try to keep pensioner poverty at bay, while keeping a close eye on the soaring cost of providing state pensions.

One benefit introduced to lessen pensioner poverty is Pension Credit, a means-tested payout made to people aged 60 or over (rising to 65 by 2020). In effect, Pension Credit tops up a pensioner's income so that it reaches a certain minimum threshold. In the 2008/09 tax year, this weekly income threshold is £124.05 (£6451 a year) for single people and £189.35 (£9846 a year) for couples.

The big problem with Pension Credit is that it is means-tested, which means that your entitlement to it is affected by your income and any savings over £6000. What's more, it is not paid automatically, but must be claimed individually by pensioners. Thanks to these hurdles, it is estimated that up to six out of 10 pensioners (58%) don't claim this and other means-tested benefits. Indeed, the charity Age Concern calculates that, each year, pensioners miss out on £4.6 billion of benefits to which they are entitled.

To learn more about (and apply for) pension credit, visit *www.thepensionservice.gov.uk/pensioncredit* or call 0800 991234.

Company pensions

If you work for an organisation with no more than four employees, then your employer is not obliged to offer you any form of company pension. However, businesses with five or more employees must offer some form of pension provision, with the minimum being a 'stakeholder' scheme (see below).

Generally speaking, joining a company or occupational pension scheme at the earliest opportunity is usually your best bet. This is because many employers make extra contributions on your behalf, provide extra benefits and bear the cost of administering the scheme.

Company pensions can be divided into two types.

Defined-benefit (also known as final-salary) schemes

Members of a defined-benefit company pension receive pensions based on their salary and the number of years they have been in the scheme. Usually, pensions are based on final salary at retirement, although some 'smoothing' over the last few years may apply. Typically, the normal retirement age will be 65, although a few generous schemes kick in at 60.

Here's a quick worked example. Let's say that you earn £24,000 a year and have been in a '1/60th' final-salary pension scheme for 30 years. Thus, for each year of service, you receive a pension worth one-sixtieth of your final salary. Thus, 30 years' service produces a pension of half of your salary, in this case, £12,000 a year.

Defined-benefit schemes are considered to be the 'gold standard' of company pensions. They usually provide generous benefits and guarantees to employees, such as index-linked pensions (which increase every year), spouse's pensions (for widows or widowers), ill-health pensions, and 'death in service' cover (life insurance for members). However, employers take on most of the costs and risks of providing such schemes, with workers' contributions being relatively modest in comparison. The average employer contribution to a defined-benefit scheme is a whopping 22% of salary.

Hence, many employers have responded by closing down or restricting access to these top-notch pension schemes. Others have reduced the benefits on offer, increased their normal retirement age, or hiked contribution rates from employees in order to cover growing financial shortfalls. Therefore, you should not give up membership of a final-salary pension scheme without a fight, as it is one of the rarest and most valuable employee benefits available!

Defined-contribution (also known as money-purchase) schemes

The size of a defined-contribution company pension depends on three things: how much you and your employer pay in, the charges deducted, and the investment returns that these contributions earn over time. Obviously, the higher the contributions, the lower the charges, and the greater the investment returns, the larger your final pot will be.

Note that it is usual for both employers and employees to make contributions into money-purchase schemes. Normally, employees contribute a fixed percentage of salary each month, say, 5% to 10%. The typical employer contribution into a defined-contribution pension scheme is a mere 6% of annual salary, not much more than a quarter of that paid into a typical defined-benefit scheme.

When you retire, part of your fund – usually no more than a quarter (25%) – can be withdrawn as a tax-free cash sum. The remainder is then used to provide you with an income, normally by buying what's known as an annuity (see below). The bad news is that normally this income is taxable so, even after retiring following a lifetime of work, you could still end up paying tax on your pensions. However, you do not have to pay National Insurance Contributions (NICs) on income from pensions.

In addition, employees who wish to boost their pension can pay extra sums into their company pension, known as additional voluntary contributions (AVCs). Generally, these AVCs are invested into a money-purchase plan, although some final-salary schemes (largely in the public sector) do allow members to use extra contributions to buy added years or additional benefits.

Before April 2006, it was not normally possible to continue working for an employer after starting to receive an income from your employer's pension scheme. However, since A-Day, this is no problem, provided your scheme trustees have introduced this change. Of course, this puts an end to the 'all or nothing' approach to working, and allows employees gradually to 'phase in' their retirement.

Once again, it's worth mentioning how much more attractive final-salary schemes are than money-purchase schemes. The average employer contribution into a defined-benefit scheme is almost 16% of annual salary. For defined-contribution schemes, the average is under 6%. Indeed, if you are fortunate enough to be in a non-contributory final-salary scheme (the cream of the crop), then this benefit could be costing your employer a quarter (25%) of your salary!

Personal (private) pensions

If you are self-employed, or your employer does not offer a decent company pension, then your next option is to find – and fund – your own pension. Although personal pensions have been around for decades, improved regulation, reduced charges and greater choice have made this market far more competitive. As a consequence, consumers can choose from hundreds of differently branded pension plans, although these generally fall into these three categories.

Personal pensions

All personal pensions are money-purchase plans, where your contributions are invested over the long term in order to build a pot which can then be used to buy a retirement income. Sometimes, an employer will agree to pay into an employee's personal pension, but this is usually down to individual negotiation.

Normally, your contributions will be paid into an investment fund managed by a life insurance company or other asset manager. Contributions from a large number of customers are pooled and then invested in a wide range of assets, such as shares, property, bonds and cash. Of course, the plan manager demands a fee for this service – and hefty fees will have a significant negative impact on your investment returns in the long run.

Stakeholder pensions

One problem with personal pensions is that high charges and inferior investment returns have left many of their owners feeling very disappointed. Thus, in an attempt to improve the public perception of personal pensions, the government introduced a new type of personal pension.

In April 2001, the government unveiled low-cost 'stakeholder' pensions, which were simpler and more flexible than traditional private pensions. Unlike many old-style personal pensions, stakeholder pensions allow customers to increase, decrease, start and stop contributions without penalty. In addition, minimum contributions are very low, with £20 being the smallest possible payment.

Furthermore, stakeholder pensions have no initial charges and annual management charges were initially capped at 1% a year. However, stakeholder pensions set up after 5 April 2005 can charge as much as 1.5% a year for the first 10 years, reducing to 1% thereafter. So, stakeholder pensions can be viewed as 'cheap and cheerful' personal pensions.

Stakeholder pensions were particularly aimed at workers earning between £10,000 and £20,000 a year without access to company pensions. However, take-up by these workers has been relatively low, so the stakeholder idea has yet to achieve its wider goals. Nevertheless, the introduction of these low-cost pensions has put pressure on other personal pensions, helping to reduce charges across the market. So, in this respect, stakeholders have been a relative success.

❝ the introduction of these low-cost pensions has put pressure on other personal pensions ❞

Self-invested personal pensions (SIPPs)

Although self-invested personal pensions (SIPPs) have been around since 1989, they have only gained significant ground in the past five years. A SIPP can be described as a 'do it yourself' pension, because you make all the decisions required to manage your plan. Indeed, a SIPP is merely a tax-free 'wrapper' surrounding investments which you choose and manage. If you wish, you can engage the help of investment managers and professional advisers, or go it alone.

Thanks to their high charges, early SIPPs were viewed as a niche product for wealthy investors. However, as fees have tumbled and demand has risen, SIPPs have grown more popular, especially since A-Day. Today, SIPPs are very much a mass-market product, thanks to the freedom, control and flexibility which they provide. For example, it is possible to put business premises into a SIPP, in order to benefit from tax-free capital gains and rental income.

Furthermore, you can now build an ultra-low-cost pension inside a SIPP. Providers such as Hargreaves Lansdown and Fidelity allow investors to create a pension portfolio based around low-cost funds with total charges under 0.5% a year. These bargain SIPPs are proving very popular with investors who are keen on a low-cost, no-nonsense approach to retirement saving.

Switching between pensions can make sense

Although it's generally not a good idea to leave or transfer out of a final-salary company pension, there are benefits to be had from transferring between personal pensions. For example, you could switch your existing pot and future contributions from a high-charging, traditional personal pension into a low-cost stakeholder pension or SIPP.

By reducing your ongoing management fees, you will boost your investment returns and, all other things being equal, this will produce a larger final pot. Another benefit of transferring pensions to a new provider is that you can put all of your existing pensions 'under one roof', making them easier to monitor and manage. Then again, breaking free of an existing pension contract may mean paying some form of exit penalty. Therefore, before you go down this route, consult a firm with specific experience of pension transfers.

Creating a pensions CV

Few of us will work for a single employer throughout the course of our entire working life. Hence, most of us end up with a jumble of pensions from different sources. To get to grips with your historical pensions, create a 'pensions CV' which lists all of your periods of service with different employers. This will do two things. First, you can identify any gaps in your pension history which may need to be cancelled out through extra contributions. Second, using your pensions CV, you should contact the trustees of each scheme in order to confirm your pension entitlement on retirement.

If you have any trouble finding a former employer or pension trustees then contact the Pension Tracing Service at *www.thepensionservice.gov.uk/atoz/atozdetailed/pensiontracing.asp*.

Forecasting your pensions

If you want to know how much you are likely to receive from your current company pension, then speak to your personnel or HR department. Likewise, to obtain a pension forecast from a previous scheme, contact your former employer or the pension trustees. You should receive a yearly pension statement from these firms, but this contact can be broken if you fail to notify an organisation of your change of address.

Likewise, you should receive a yearly pension forecast from any existing or previous personal pensions. In addition, by plugging some figures into the pension calculator at *www.pensioncalculator.org.uk*, you can get a rough idea of what your current pension plan might produce in terms of income.

Furthermore, to obtain a forecast for your state pensions, you need to complete and return a BR19 form which can be obtained by calling 0845 3000 168 or from the Pension Service website at *www.thepensionservice.gov.uk/resourcecentre/br19/home.asp*.

Choosing a pension

When it comes to state pensions, you have limited choice – you receive the pension that the state wishes to pay you. Given that financial legislation constantly evolves, it's almost impossible to say how much your state pension will be worth decades from now. With company pensions, your options will be fairly restricted, but you may be able to choose from several schemes for employees.

However, with personal and stakeholder pensions and SIPPs, there is a huge choice of plans from which to choose. It's almost impossible to say which personal pension plan will suit you best, because this very much depends on your personal situation. In particular, your current age, the age at which you wish to retire, your contribution levels, and your attitude to risk will all have an effect on your choice of plan.

Nevertheless, all other things being equal, it's a good idea to choose a plan with modest management charges. Indeed, over time, paying an annual management charge of 0.75% instead of 1.5% will have a major impact on the value of your final pension pot. Hence, it's important to look long and hard at the charging structure of pensions before picking one. Fortunately, you can check these charges at the Financial Services Authority website: *www.fsa.gov.uk/tables*.

Your options at retirement

Unless you're in a final-salary scheme, your pension contributions build up during your working life to create a pot of money to be used to provide you with a pension. Some of this pot can be withdrawn as tax-free cash (see below), but how do you turn the remainder into income?

Annuities

By handing over your pension pot to a life insurance company, you can buy a lifetime income known as an annuity. In exchange for this lump sum, the insurer guarantees to pay you an income for the rest of your life. Alas, the big problem with annuities is that, once handed over, your pension pot is gone forever.

Thus, an annuity is a gamble by a life insurer on how long it expects an annuitant to live. If you live longer than the life company expects, then the gamble goes your way. However, if you die earlier than expected, then the life assurer wins the bet.

The annuity income that you receive depends on a number of personal factors. These include your age, gender (as women live longer than men), smoker status, marital status and state of health. In addition, this income will be affected by financial factors, such as the general level of interest rates, and whether you choose a level or index-linked annuity (one which rises over time).

Another problem with annuities is that they depend on long-term interest rates. As interest rates have dropped considerably since the early Nineties, annuity rates have declined to about half of their previous level. Furthermore, as life expectancy increases, annuity rates fall. Hence, it is absolutely vital to shop around for the best-value annuity before you hand over your pension pot.

As the pricing of annuities becomes more sophisticated, life insurers are increasingly tailoring annuities using individual pricing, in order to improve the accuracy of the 'annuity gamble'. Hence, if you are a smoker, in poor health or have a condition which is likely to shorten your life, then you should investigate the possibility of buying an 'impaired life' annuity. As your annuity is likely to be paid over a shorter time span, an impaired-life annuity provides a higher yearly income.

It's vital to understand that you do not have to buy an annuity from the pension provider with which you (or your employer) have saved. In fact, companies are obliged to inform you of your legal right to buy an annuity from the company of your choice.

Despite the existence of this 'open market option', only two in five customers (40%) bother to compare annuity rates before making this once-in-a-lifetime decision. Sadly, failing to shop around for a Best Buy annuity could mean losing thousands of pounds during the later years of your life. On the other hand, doing your homework could boost your retirement income by up to 30% for the remainder of your life.

You can learn more about annuities at *www.hlannuity.co.uk.*

Income drawdown: an alternative to annuities

As I mentioned earlier, annuity rates have slipped sharply over the past decade, in line with long-term interest rates. For instance, a £100,000 pension pot may have bought you a yearly income of £10,000 in the early Nineties. Today, your annuity income might only be half as much.

Thus, some investors are not willing to lock into an annuity while rates are low. Instead, they have opted for a pension income via 'income drawdown'. Although income drawdown is riskier than buying a guaranteed annuity for life, it does offer greater flexibility.

With income drawdown, you leave your money in your pension pot and simply draw an income from the fund each year. This income is subject to minimum and maximum limits laid down in law. So, with income drawdown, your money remains invested and will rise or fall in line with the value of the assets in your fund. Hence, your fund can continue to grow (or shrink) free of tax inside your pension.

Thus, a fall in the stock market could see a drop in both the value of, and the income from, your pension. Hence, income drawdown is only suitable for long-term investors who can afford to take some risk with their pension fund. Investors who are not willing to see the value of their pension pot and retirement income vary over time would be safer buying an annuity.

If you die during income drawdown then your pension pot can be paid to your beneficiaries, less a tax penalty of 35%.

Alternatively, your pot can be used to provide an income to your dependants. However, from the age of 75, you can no longer continue with income drawdown. Even so, you can continue to take an income from your pension fund, known as an 'alternatively secured pension', or ASP. After your death, your ASP must be used to provide an income for your dependants. If you have no dependants, then your fund can be left to charity free of Inheritance Tax.

Insured retirement plans: a halfway house

Ever keen to come up with new-fangled financial products, insurers have imported a US-style retirement plan which combines elements of both annuities and income drawdown. Three US firms (MetLife, Hartford and Lincoln) dominate the market for these 'insured retirement plans', with Dutch firm Aegon the latest entrant.

You can buy an insured retirement plan (IRP) at any age between 55 and 70, and convert it to a conventional annuity by the required age of 75. Before this time, your money remains invested, usually in shares and other assets. The big difference between an IRP and income drawdown is that you receive a guaranteed minimum income. Also, if your fund increases in value, then your monthly income could rise.

Although IRPs sound like a revolutionary idea, combining an income guarantee with potential growth, they fall down in one respect. Their charges can cut your investment returns by up to 1.6% a year, which is a fairly steep price to pay for the comfort of a guaranteed, but modest, income.

Thus, IRPs are really aimed at experienced, long-term investors who are prepared to take a view on charges, investment returns and life expectancy. Indeed, anyone with a pension fund worth less than £100,000 should probably disregard IRPs and look elsewhere.

Tax-free cash

All money-purchase, personal and stakeholder pensions (and some company pensions) allow you to withdraw up to a quarter (25%) of your pension fund as a tax-free lump sum. Since April 2006, you can withdraw your 25% tax-free cash from additional voluntary contributions (see above) and from pensions used to contract-out of the State Second Pension/SERPS.

Of course, by saving or investing this money, you can use it to generate additional retirement income through savings interest, share dividends, etc. Another option is to use your tax-free cash to buy a tax-efficient income in the form of a purchased life annuity (PLA). The advantage of using your own money to buy an annuity is that you only pay tax on part of this income. This is because your money is treated as though it were returned to you over a 20-year period. Hence, only income in excess of 5% a year is subject to income tax.

For the record, annuity rates on purchased life annuities are slightly lower than those paid by annuities bought using pension funds. This is because insurance companies believe that only people in good health would use their own money to buy annuities. However, after taking tax into account, PLAs produce higher incomes than standard annuities.

By the way, although you can recycle your tax-free cash into an ISA or other investment vehicle, HMRC rules prevent you from putting this lump sum back into a pension in order to grab another round of tax relief!

Trivial commutation

If the total value of all of your personal and company pension pots is under a certain level (£16,500 in the 2008/09 tax year), then you can opt to take these small pensions in cash. In order to do this, you must be aged between 60 and 75. Although a quarter of this will be tax free, the remaining 75% will be taxed. Closing down your pensions in this way is known as 'trivial commutation'. Note that a company scheme may not allow you to do this if the trustees have not introduced this rule.

The pitfalls of pensions

By now, I hope you can see that, thanks to tax relief on contributions, pensions provide a worthy tax shelter for retirement saving. On the other hand, thanks to their limitations, pensions are far from perfect.

Indeed, pensions are remarkably inflexible investment vehicles. For example, your money can be locked in for decades, because you cannot access your pension pots until you reach 55 (50 if taken before the 2010/11 tax year). Furthermore, you may be obliged to convert the bulk of your pension pot into an annuity at a time when rates are low.

Thus, although pensions will probably form the bedrock of your retirement planning, they are not the only option open to you. Some investors dislike the relative rigidity of pensions, preferring instead to save inside tax-free ISAs or by investing directly in shares. Others prefer the attraction of buy-to-let property as a means of securing their pension.

Thus, my advice would be not to put your entire faith in pensions, as the tax treatment of investments will change over time. By adopting a portfolio or 'pick and mix' approach to investing for retirement, you can spread your risk and improve the flexibility of your retirement options.

In addition, remember that you may not need a bumper pension to enjoy a comfortable retirement. After working life ends, many of your expenses will be lower. For a start, it's likely that you will be mortgage-free, and there will be none of the expenses associated with daily commuting. Indeed, you may find that you can live comfortably in retirement on less than half your former salary.

The future of pensions: Personal Accounts

Both membership of, and contributions to, pensions have tumbled since the turn of the century. Hence, the government is concerned that many workers are not doing enough to fund their retirement adequately.

Thus, from 2012, the government intends to introduce a new form of work-based pensions known as Personal Accounts. All eligible workers aged between 22 and state retirement age will be able to save in a pension with compulsory contributions from their employer.

All workers would automatically be enrolled into a Personal Accounts scheme or an occupational scheme which is at least as attractive. Of course, automatic enrolment won't apply to workers already in a good-quality workplace pension, who will simply stay put. However, workers who feel that the Personal Accounts scheme isn't right for them can actively opt out.

The idea of Personal Accounts is to offer a simple, low-cost pension plan to modestly paid workers who don't have access to an occupational pension scheme. To persuade workers to join Personal Accounts, employers will be made to contribute a minimum of 3% of earnings to employees' pensions. On top of this, employees can contribute a further 4%, which then attracts tax relief of around 1%. In total, this comes to 8% of salary, which is a decent start to saving for retirement.

For more information on Personal Accounts, visit *www.dwp.gov. uk/pensionsreform/new_way.asp*.

A final word on women and pensions

❝ while the majority of men receive the full state pension, fewer than half of all female pensioners do ❞

Women live longer, earn less and spend fewer years in the workforce than men do. Thus, for the female half of the population, pensions can be especially problematic. For instance, while the majority of men receive the full state pension, fewer than half of all female pensioners do. Also, all women born after 5 April 1978 will not receive their state pension until they reach age 68.

Thus, for women, starting early and saving hard is essential in order to maintain a decent standard of living in retirement. Relying on a 'knight in shining armour' to bail you out is not a sensible option!

8

Steering clear of scams

In the first seven chapters of this book, you've discovered how to make, manage and hang onto more money. In this final chapter, you will learn how to avoid having it stolen from under your nose.

Long before money was invented as payment for goods and services, there were dishonest people keen to swindle the unwary, gullible and greedy. Indeed, 'scam culture' has become deeply embedded in human society. The proof is in the long list of synonyms for scams and scamming: cheat, con, deceive, defraud, dupe, fiddle, fleece, hoodwink, rip off, swindle, trick and so on.

Thanks to advancements in modern communications, especially the Internet, we're all at the mercy of millions of fraudsters, cheats and hoaxers around the globe. It's a fact that, without a good spam filter, your email inbox will quickly become full of 'get rich quick' schemes.

Hence, it is vital to recognise and avoid a whole host of sophisticated scams and swindles. In this section, I have listed 22 scams to dodge. However, thanks to the cunning and ingenuity of scammers, no list of this kind can be all-inclusive, so do keep your wits about you.

How to recognise a scam

Although no two swindles are exactly alike, they often have certain hallmarks. Watch out for any of the following:

- Scams usually arrive via unsolicited emails, telephone calls, letters or faxes.

- Generally, they ask for money upfront in return for delivering a windfall, lump sum, prize or inheritance.

- They promise returns far beyond the 6% a year you could make in a good savings account.

- They rarely explain how these fantastic returns will be generated.

- They claim secret or 'inside' knowledge (always the 'bait' for gambling and boiler-room scams).

- They promise huge or instant rewards for little effort.

- They rely on roping in more and more people in order to continue operating.

- They never explain why you have been specially selected for this golden opportunity.

Thus, in the words of the old saying, 'If it looks too good to be true, then it almost always is'.

Now let's examine some of the most common swindles in operation in the UK. For further information on scams, visit the Office of Fair Trading's Scambuster website at *www.oft.gov.uk/Consumer/Scams/default.htm*.

Advance-fee fraud

We begin with a look at the most common and successful scam: advance-fee fraud, which may well be 'the oldest trick in the book'.

Advance-fee fraud is remarkably simple: a swindler demands money upfront with the promise of riches further down the line. Typically, you are promised a huge payout (sometimes amounting to millions of pounds) in return for a one-off fee. Of course, once you've paid this upfront charge, the conman disappears and you lose both your promised fortune and your own hard-earned cash.

One well-known variant of advance-fee fraud is known as the 'Nigerian' or '419' scam (after the relevant section of the Nigerian penal code). An email from an overseas official or politician promises you untold wealth in return for your assistance with spiriting away illicit funds from his home country. As a reward for your services (and the use of your bank account), you receive, say, a 25% share of a multi-million pound fortune.

Of course, what actually happens is that the fraudster takes your money and runs. Alternatively, armed with your banking details, he clears out the cash from your current account. Sadly, some advance-fee criminals keep coming back to milk their victims time and time again. Extra money is demanded for unforeseen expenses, such as administrative expenses, bribes for corrupt officials, customs duties, legal fees or transfer taxes. In some cases, victims are fleeced several times, sometimes sustaining losses of £100,000+.

So, if you're offered a life-changing amount in return for handing over a smaller amount then don't be suckered into parting with your cash. Don't let greed override your common sense. Otherwise, you are sure to become yet another victim of advance-fee fraud, which could lead to you losing your life savings!

Bogus property investments

During the property boom which began in the mid-Nineties, various property investment scams sprang up. Typically, these promise high, guaranteed returns to investors willing to pump money into buy-to-let properties.

One infamous example was Practical Property Portfolio (PPP), which promised returns of 15% a year in return for investments of £18,000+. PPP claims to use investors' money to buy properties to be refurbished and then let to social tenants at a guaranteed rent.

Although it may have been possible to make such returns during the peak years of the property boom, this was not the case with PPP. Usually, the properties purchased turned out to be worth very much less than their valuations. Furthermore, any 'rent guarantees' proved to be pie in the sky.

After numerous complaints to Trading Standards, PPP was raided by the police in March 2003. A year later, the Department of Trade and Industry wound up PPP and 10 associated companies in the High Court. Alas, its victims lost tens of millions of pounds while PPP's owners were raking in their ill-gotten gains. Once again, the promise of high returns with no risk proved to be false.

It's important to note that direct investments in property are not regulated by the Financial Services Authority (FSA). Thus, you're not protected by the safety net provided by the Financial Services Compensation Scheme (FSCS) and cannot claim compensation when the roof caves in.

Boiler rooms

One very dangerous swindle is the 'boiler room' share scam. This begins with a telephone call or email from a smooth-talking salesman. He offers you 'an investment opportunity of a lifetime' to make mega-returns in a little-known 'hot stock'. Although his sales patter may sound convincing, he's selling nothing more than snake oil.

Alas, both innocent and experienced investors have been conned into buying shares in fictional or worthless businesses. In almost every case, boiler rooms are located outside of the UK (Spain is a popular location) and not governed by the Financial Services Authority. Thus, any losses sustained as a result of these 'share tips from hell' will not be governed by the Financial Services Compensation Scheme. In some cases, unsuspecting victims have lost £50,000+ before realising that their 'dead cert' investment is really a dead duck!

So, don't allow a persuasive salesman to con you into buying ropey shares through playing on fear, greed and flattery. In fact,

" don't listen to unwanted sales pitches about investment, no matter how plausible "

don't listen to unwanted sales pitches about investment, no matter how plausible the caller or company sounds. The safest thing to do is to use your common sense, hang up and walk away. This is a get-rich-quick scheme for salesmen, not investors.

To see a boiler room in action, watch *Boiler Room*, starring Vin Diesel, Giovanni Ribisi and Ben Affleck. This film thrillingly demonstrates how easy it is to sucker people out of their life savings!

Only firms regulated by the Financial Services Authority can offer investment services to the British public. Always check a firm's registration first at *www.fsa.gov.uk/register*.

Criminal cashback

This sneaky trick relies on the fact that electronic money transfers travel faster than cheques. Let's say that you place an advert in your local newspaper in order to sell your car. A buyer duly appears, but he sends you a cheque or banker's draft for a sum greater than your asking price. The bogus buyer asks you to bank this cheque and then send the excess to him by money transfer.

The problem is that your money transfer takes immediate effect and is irreversible, whereas his fake cheque or banker's draft will 'bounce' (be returned unpaid) a few days later. Of course, when you try to track down the phoney borrower, he is nowhere to be found, leaving you heavily out of pocket. For more advice on criminal cashback, read this fraud alert from the Metropolitan Police: *www.met.police.uk/fraudalert/section/cashback_fraud.htm*.

Dodgy share-trading software

Any private investor with a few years' experience will tell you that there is no sure-fire formula guaranteed to make money on the stock market. In spite of this, you will see lots of adverts for share-trading software packages which claim to produce market-beating returns.

Of course, the Holy Grail of investing is to produce superior returns with no risk. Alas, this is a mirage, as even the world's most powerful traders and investment banks sometimes come a cropper. Let's be honest, if you came up with a guaranteed way to win with shares, you'd keep it to yourself, right?

Alternatively, you could sell it to the highest bidder and retire to your own private beach. The last thing you would do would be to share your 'inside secrets' with the great unwashed! Yet again, share-trading software is yet another example of a scheme to enrich the seller, rather than the buyer.

Fake invoices, bogus business directories, and dodgy data protection services

(Although these scams are commonly aimed at businesses, we should all watch out for them.)

Many British businesses are bombarded with demands for payment for unsolicited or unwanted goods and services. The most common scam is to send a demand for payment for a service which is either worthless or non-existent.

For example, when data protection laws changed a few years ago, small businesses were flooded with offers of data protection services. In almost every case, these data protection firms charge high fees for a service which was available either free or at low cost. Very quickly, this grew to become the biggest business trick in the UK. However, with the passage of time, it is no longer as widespread as it once was.

An even simpler trick is to send a wholly fake invoice to a business for services allegedly provided. For instance, an invoice for stationery for a modest sum might slip under the radar and be paid without further investigation. Although most established companies have procedures in place to monitor outgoing payments, fake invoices are sometimes paid by mistake.

Hence, the fake invoice scam relies on disorganised, unwary or busy workers not doing their job properly. The initial invoice may be followed up by threats of referral to debt collectors, court action or credit blacklisting. However, you should never be bullied into paying for goods or services that you did not order or were never delivered.

Another major scam aimed at businesses, especially small firms and sole traders, is the bogus 'business directory'. Naturally, small businesses are keen to promote their services to the public. Fraudsters play on this by urging businesses to sign up to a business directory which promises to promote their services across the whole of the UK or Europe.

The usual trick is to approach businesses by email or telephone, inviting them to appear in a directory or listings website. Sometimes, the cost of advertising in these bogus directories is tucked away in the small print. Of course, the fee demanded far outweighs any publicity received. Indeed, it's often the case that the directory doesn't even exist. The fees for these services can often amount to several hundred pounds, and failure to pay the invoice usually leads to additional penalties.

Today, bogus business directories are the biggest business-to-business swindle in the UK. If you believe that you have fallen victim to such a scam then contact your local Trading Standards office. Under the *Business Protection from Misleading Marketing Regulations 2008*, which came into force in May 2008, the law protects you against UK-based companies promoting misleading business directories.

Unfortunately, many of these scams are run from abroad, so don't be fooled or cajoled into signing up with anyone other than the well-known business directories, such as Yellow Pages or Thomson Local. Also, don't be intimidated into paying a bogus invoice by threats of legal action. In 99% of cases, these threats are hollow, as the last thing fraudsters wish to see is the inside of a courtroom! In summary, the best advice is to avoid the problem in the first place.

❝ the best advice is to avoid the problem in the first place ❞

Fake lotteries

Since its launch in November 1994, the Lotto has grown to become a national obsession. Hence, fraudsters now use the British obsession with 'jackpot fever' to rip off the unwary.

If you receive an email or telephone call informing you that you've won a prize in a foreign lottery then delete the email or hang up. Of course, we all know that you can't win a lottery without entering by buying a ticket. Thus, the 'bogus lottery win' is yet another variation on advance-fee fraud.

Before you can claim your 'prize', a pretend lottery official will ask you for money to cover taxes, insurance, administration and customs charges. Alas, any money you hand over will be lost for ever, as your promised king's ransom is nothing more than a fantasy. Alas, four in five victims of lottery scams are over 65, as the villains in overseas call centres specifically target the elderly and vulnerable. Hence, most victims are too ashamed to come forward and report their loss.

Fishing for cash

Another phone-based scam aims to relieve you of your cash by obtaining details of your plastic cards or bank account. A crook claiming to be from the fraud detection department of a bank, MasterCard or VISA claims that there has been some unusual spending activity on your account.

The caller takes down your card number and other details, including the three-digit security code (the CVV2, or card verification value) on the back of your card. Using this information, together with your name and address, the criminal can then embark on a spending spree paid for with your plastic. So, never divulge any financial or personal information to callers. Instead, hang up and call your bank using the usual 'lost or stolen' emergency number.

Gambling syndicates

Paying to join a 'gambling syndicate' or 'betting ring' – either by buying 'beat the bookie' tips or tipping software – is sure to leave you nursing heavy losses. In many ways, these tipping services are similar to computerised share-trading packages, in that they promise a 'foolproof system' which simply cannot deliver.

One infamous example of this gambling fiddle was the KF Concept, named after Kevin Foster, a former cabbie from Kent. After a lengthy investigation, KF Concept was closed down by the FSA, but not before 8500 'investors' lost tens of millions of pounds. Mr Foster was declared bankrupt in 2005 with debts of £36 million. He now faces numerous criminal charges, following an investigation by the Serious Fraud Office.

If you want to become rich through gambling then buy shares in a bookmaker, or open your own betting shop or casino!

Home-working scams

Home-working scams claim to offer a high income for very little effort. Often, these involve some kind of repetitive activity, such as stuffing envelopes or manufacturing small items. The scam involves paying an upfront fee, only to find that it is nearly impossible to receive payment for the goods or services you produce.

Seven out of 10 workers in the UK earn under £25,000 a year, which comes to around £12.50 an hour before deductions. All well-paid jobs involve some degree of education, experience, hard work, risk, skill – or criminality. Hence, it's highly unlikely that you can earn high wages for little effort, especially by working at home.

Although there are established direct-selling or network-marketing businesses (such as Avon, Betterware or Kleeneze), home-working scams promise a great deal and deliver very little or nothing. So, if you're interested in starting your own business, then take advice from a reputable organisation such as Business Link, see *www.businesslink.gov.uk*.

Identity theft and fraud

Thanks to the huge popularity of telephone and online banking, there is now a whole host of scams designed to steal your financial details and, later, plunder your bank or credit card account. In particular, there has been massive growth in 'phishing' scams – emails or telephone calls from criminals keen to hack into your bank account (see Phishing emails and calls, page 181).

In addition, some burglars have moved from stealing consumer goods to taking financial documents that can be used to commit identity fraud. After all, your new DVD player may fetch less than £50 on the black market. However, armed with your identity, a criminal can obtain thousands of pounds of credit in your name.

66 armed with your identity, a criminal can obtain thousands of pounds 99

So, in order to protect your money, you must safeguard your personal and financial data. Never let your plastic cards out of your sight, especially in restaurants and petrol stations. Otherwise, your card may be 'skimmed' and, together with your PIN, used to run up enormous debts in your name. Also, use a confetti-style shredder to destroy any paperwork containing personal or financial details. Of course, you should never give out financial information (especially account numbers and passwords) by telephone or email.

Inheritance scams

Again, this is a simple twist on advance-fee fraud, with the promised payout being an inheritance from a long-lost relative or family friend. Although many inheritance scams originate overseas, particularly in other English-speaking countries, some originate from the UK. So, don't be tempted to hand over money to a bogus lawyer in the hope of receiving a miracle windfall.

Land-banking swindles

This hoax relies on the British obsession with ever-rising property and land prices. A land-banking company sells small plots of land to investors, claiming that their value will soar when the area is sold to developers. Usually, there are two problems with these parcels of land. First, they do not have planning permission and are unlikely to be granted it. Second, they are often in 'green belt' areas or other parts of the British countryside which are highly likely to remain fields.

So, by buying into a land-banking scheme, you are handing over large sums of money in order to buy a patch of grass in the middle of nowhere. Indeed, in June 2008, the FSA acted to close down the UK's largest illegal land-banking scheme, run by UKLI Limited, or 'United Kingdom Land Investments'. It appears that about 4500 investors have bought 5000 plots of land, and stand to lose up to £69 million.

Make a Million seminars

One of the best ways to 'get rich quick' is to promote seminars which promise to make the man in the street a millionaire within a few years. Typically, investors will visit a hotel in order to hear a free presentation from a property or investment 'guru'. However, the real money is made by selling follow-up workshops, promising insider information at, say, £2500 per head.

Usually, the quality of information provided on these courses is no better than you'd find in a good book on the subject. Yet again, the only people to get rich from these courses are the organisers, who make thousands of pounds a day for sharing their false 'wisdom' with mere mortals. So, this is yet another dead end, rather than a rapid road to riches.

Multi-level-marketing programmes

YOU could earn £75,000 a year from our unique multi-level-marketing programme!

Although you could earn a living wage from direct selling, it often involves long hours for little reward. Frequently, these promises fail to live up to their hype, leaving new recruits or franchisees out of pocket, thanks to ongoing membership fees or upfront investments. As always, you take a great risk by parting with money in advance.

Phishing emails and calls

Every day, all over the world, email inboxes are clogged up with spam – unwanted and unsolicited messages. Amongst the most dangerous spam are 'phishing' ('fishing') emails, which seek to steal your bank or credit card details. Typically, they take the form of an email from your bank which asks for confidential information in order to verify that your account is safe. Any information (especially passwords) which you provide will be used to hack into your accounts in order to empty them as soon as possible.

Never respond to any of these emails and never click on any links within them. Otherwise, you will be directed to a fake (but identical) copy of your bank's website. Instead, set up your spam filter to remove all such messages, and make sure that your computer security is up to date. Likewise, never give out confidential information to telephone callers.

For more advice on keeping your online finances secure, visit the Bank Safe Online website at *www.banksafeonline.org.uk*.

Ponzi, pyramid and matrix schemes

In 1920, plenty of Americans were taken in by a swindler called Charles Ponzi. Ponzi promised 50% returns to investors, turning $100 into $150 within 45 days. Although Ponzi claimed to be trading in 'postal coupons', in fact, he used contributions from new investors to pay fake gains to earlier investors. As one judge remarked, 'His scheme was simply the old fraud of paying the earlier comers out of the contributions of the later comers'.

Ponzi's pyramid scheme became so infamous that his name is now used to describe similar 'pyramid' schemes where new money is recycled as bogus returns to previous investors. These scams rely on recruiting more and more people in order to generate the alleged gains. There is no investment to earn returns, nor any products or services to sell. When there is little or no explanation of how returns are made, your suspicions should be aroused. Normally, all that happens is that money changes hands between 'winners' and 'losers'.

Following huge losses sustained by Britons in pyramid schemes such as *Hearts* and *Women Empowering Women*, most pyramid or matrix schemes have been outlawed. However, they will always persist, so watch out for make-believe schemes which promise handsome returns, yet rely on recruiting ever-greater numbers of participants.

Obviously, as these illegal and unregulated pyramid schemes grow, they need to suck in more and more punters in order to keep going. For example, let's say that each new entrant must find eight new recruits in order to trigger a payout. In turn, these people must each find eight victims, and so on. For the 11th round of recruiting to succeed, a total of 8.59 billion people are required, which is more than the entire population of the Earth (6.7 billion).

So, as you can see, 'pyramid' money-making schemes are founded on sand, and are thus doomed to fail!

Premium-rate telephone lines and scratchcard scams

Beware of competitions which encourage you to call a premium-rate number in order to claim your winnings. The most common scam of this form involves scratchcards which are posted through your letterbox or fall out of newspapers. (Don't confuse these with genuine National Lottery scratchcards sold by retailers.) Usually, these dodgy scratchcards require you to make a lengthy call to a 090 number which charges £1.50 a minute. For example, claiming your prize may involve a six-minute phone call costing £9, in order to receive a prize worth a fraction of this.

Sham charities

Before donating goods or contributing money to a charity, make sure that it is genuine. Many areas have been targeted by bogus charity collectors seeking old clothes, toys and other goods. Often, these are commercial companies that leaflet whole areas, aiming to make a profit by recycling textiles and other materials by the tonne.

Also, watch out for fake charity collectors who collect door-to-door or in streets and pubs. If you want to help good causes, make sure that you donate to a registered charity. For more advice, read this warning from the Charity Commission: *www.gnn.gov.uk/content/detail.asp?ReleaseID=250630&NewsAreaID =2&NavigatedFromSearch=True.*

Share-buyback frauds

This is a sophisticated version of the ages-old advance-fee fraud. It seems to happen most often to investors in small companies, particularly those whose share prices have fallen to a fraction of their former highs.

The fraudster uses public records to obtain the details of shareholders in a particular company. He then calls shareholders, offering to buy their shares for many times the market price. For example, he might offer £1 for a share currently trading at 5p. Investors nursing large losses will be delighted to receive such a call from a 'strategic investor' or 'fund manager' offering such an amazing price out of the blue.

Of course, there is a fee for joining this exclusive group of key shareholders who stand to make 20 times their money. Before selling their shares, investors need to hand over a 'buyout fee' which can sometimes exceed the market value of their investment. Of course, once the fee is paid, the sham investor disappears and the conmen move on to their next victims. Thanks to recent stock market volatility, share-buyback scams have become a popular sideline for boiler rooms.

Timeshare frauds

Frankly, the timeshare market is riddled with fraud, most of which revolves around advance-fee scams. Many of these frauds are masterminded in Mediterranean countries, where legitimate timeshare activities are concentrated.

One of the biggest scams is aimed at timeshare owners who wish to sell their stake. They are approached with an offer far in excess of the value of the timeshare, in return for payment of a finder's fee. Unsurprisingly, once the finder's fee (which sometimes amounts to thousands of pounds) has been paid, both broker and buyer disappear, never to be seen again.

For more information on the many and varied timeshare scams, visit *www.timeshare.org.uk/scams.html*.

Viruses and Trojan

Lastly, it is crucial that you take the necessary steps to ensure that your home and work computers are safe to use. Without the necessary security software, your PC is at risk from infection by viruses, rogue webpages, dodgy links, spyware and spam email. So, be sure to install anti-virus, anti-spyware and firewall packages, and check for updates at least weekly.

For more advice on online security, visit *www.getsafeonline.org*.

Also, when it comes to financial security, understand that *you* are the weakest link. So, make your passwords hard to guess, and don't use the same password and username for multiple websites. Otherwise, a single slip-up could lead to all of your accounts being wiped out!

And finally . . .

❝ a fool and his money are soon parted ❞

In summary, you must learn that guarantees of easy money are nothing but empty promises. In reality, they prey on greed and ignorance, and are sure to be phoney. So, watch your step at all times, as 'a fool and his money are soon parted'. And remember: if you're at all in doubt, then don't shell out!

More advice

1 Consumer advice on scams from the Financial Services Authority: *www.moneymadeclear.fsa.gov.uk/news/scams/scams_ and_swindles.html.*

2 There is much discussion of questionable goings-on and possible financial trickery at The Motley Fool's *A Fool and His Money* discussion board: *www.boards.fool.co.uk/Messages.asp? bid=51365.*

3 The Canadian *Crimes of Persuasion* website: *www.crimes-of-persuasion.com.*

Summary and useful contacts

E arlier in this book, I likened money management to driving
a car. Continuing this theme, this is the point at which we
need to pull over, park, switch off the engine and think
about our journey. In other words, what lessons have the previous eight chapters taught us? Let's quickly run through what
we've learnt:

Cruising towards a cash-rich future

In **Chapter 1**, we started the engine and found first gear:
budgeting.

The fundamental lesson of budgeting is that what we earn isn't
as important as what we spend. Also, to have any chance of
making money our servant, we need to monitor our income and
outgoings, with the aim of maximising our disposable income.
Always remember that budgeting is the absolute foundation of
money management. Indeed, until we learn the-skills-to-pay-the-
bills, our engine stalls and our financial journey can't even begin.

In **Chapters 2 and 3**, we hit second gear: **borrowing**.

We found the golden rule of borrowing, which is to borrow as
little as we can for as short a time as we can, thus paying as little
interest as possible. Ideally, we should avoid borrowing to subsidise our lifestyle, as this sets us up for a nasty crash further
down the road. Likewise, we found out how expensive it is to
borrow using credit cards, overdrafts and so on. We then moved
on to find out how to get out of debt, using 'snowballing', free
debt-counselling services, etc.

In **Chapter 3, home-owning,** we established how best to buy the roof over our head using a mortgage. To be a happy homeowner, we need to choose a suitable, affordable home loan, while ensuring that we don't overstretch ourselves and put our home on the line. We also discovered that house prices don't always go up, which means that negative equity, arrears and repossessions are set to make an unwelcome return.

In **Chapter 4,** we found third gear, started gathering speed, and discovered the joys of **saving**.

This is where our journey started to become more enjoyable, as we move from *paying* interest to *earning* it. We found out how tax and inflation eat into savers' returns, and how to combat these twin troubles. Alas, we also realised that the UK's appetite for saving is at a 50-year low, which is a frightening prospect as an economic downturn looms. Our motto should be: *when times are good, save; when times are hard, save harder!*

In **Chapter 5,** we smoothly shifted into fourth gear and found out how to protect our assets through **insurance**.

Just as we're starting to cruise along, the last thing we want is to lose control and have a smash. So, we must insure our most valuable assets: our income, health, home, car and so on. Similarly, we found that some insurance policies are nothing more than a protection racket, such as the dreaded payment protection insurance. Swerve and avoid.

In **Chapter 6,** we moved up into fifth gear: how to build wealth through long-term **investing**.

We found out that buying shares in companies is not like gambling on a lottery ticket. Our goal is to generate extra wealth by a combination of capital growth and income. We now know that investing involves a greater degree of risk than saving, but the long-term rewards can be far greater, too .We also discovered how to minimise management fees and tax so as to increase our overall returns. Lastly, we learnt that there is no such thing as a sure-fire investment – even property investing isn't the one-way bet it pretended to be before the credit crunch.

In **Chapter 7**, we found top gear and discovered how to cruise towards a comfortable **retirement**.

Having found the fundamental tools of personal finance, we can now use these to ensure a decent standard of living when working life ends. Through a combination of state, company and personal pensions, we can invest tax-efficiently in order to build a large enough pot to see us through our old age. However, we also found that pensions aren't necessarily the be-all and end-all of retirement planning; they should form part of a larger, more comprehensive retirement safety net.

Finally, in Chapter 8, we found out how to avoid **scams**.

Having got your finances in order, the worst thing that could happen would be to have money stolen from under your nose. Wherever there's a decent-sized sum of money, there's a crowd of conmen waiting to steal it. Indeed, thousands of experienced investors have been conned by boiler rooms and their bogus promises of fabulous wealth. So, stay sharp, be cynical and always remember that *if a deal looks too good to be true, then it almost always is!*

Don't crash in the credit crunch

Congratulation on getting this far, especially if you normally find personal finance a dry subject. However, before I sign off, I want to give you one last warning.

For several years, I have warned that the UK was heading straight into a financial hurricane. We became used to spending considerably more than we earn, and funding the difference by borrowing. During the housing boom, between 1995 and 2007, savings levels dropped to lows not seen since the fifties. At the same time, property speculation was rampant, with this new-found housing wealth creating thousands of 'property millionaires'.

Today, it's quite clear that a 'live today, pay tomorrow' lifestyle is no longer an option. However you look at it, the housing bubble has burst, the debt balloon is up, credit is expensive and scarce, and so on. Financial disaster awaits those who spend too much, pay too little attention to their finances, and are unwilling to change their ways. Thus, if you want to thrive, rather than survive, for the next decade, then you need to avoid financial traffic jams and pile-ups.

Whatever economic conditions the next few years bring, the lessons and principles you take away from this book will help you to pull away from the pack in the future. There's never been a greater need for decent financial management than there is today. So, be sure to get on top of your money *before it gets on top of you*. Only then can you enjoy piece of mind and easy living.

Good decisions bring good luck

Finally, I hope that you have found this book enjoyable and easy to read. Ideally, it should act as a guidebook to help you navigate the often confusing maze that is personal finance. In time, I hope that it will also help you to make better financial decisions and, as a result, leave you much better off.

After a while, you'll start to get the hang of this money lark and, eventually, you'll have most of your financial ducks in a row. At this point, feel free to recommend this book to a friend or relative who could do with some extra help managing their money. Very few people have a firm grasp of their personal finances, so your new-found knowledge will become increasingly valuable as time goes by.

Thanks for listening!

Cliff D'Arcy
July 2008

Here are contact details of some reliable organisations that can help you to achieve your financial goals:

1 *The benefits of better budgeting*

Consumer Credit Counselling Service (CCCS): www.cccs.co.uk/budget/persbudg.aspx (a leading debt-counselling charity)

MoneySavingExpert: www.moneysavingexpert.com (the **best** site in the world when it comes to slashing your spending!)

Motley Fool: www.fool.co.uk (a wide range of advice, written in plain English)

The FSA: www.moneymadeclear.fsa.gov.uk/tools.aspx?Tool=budget_calcul ator (advice from the financial regulator)

2 *Becoming a better borrower*

CCCS: www.cccs.co.uk

Citizens Advice: www.adviceguide.org.uk (the UK's leading provider of free consumer advice)

Moneyfacts: www.moneyfacts.co.uk (the definitive guide to Best Buys and Don't Buys!)

MoneySupermarket: www.moneysupermarket.com (a leading financial comparison website)

Motley Fool: www.fool.co.uk

National Debtline: www.nationaldebtline.co.uk (another free debt-advice service)

The Samaritans: www.samaritans.org.uk (offers help when life seems hopeless)

3 *How to be a happier homeowner*

British Association of Removers: www.bar.co.uk (the trade association for removal firms)

London & Country Mortgages: www.lcplc.co.uk (a leading no-fee mortgage broker)

Moneyfacts: www.moneyfacts.co.uk/mortgages

MoneySavingExpert: www.moneysavingexpert.com/mortgages

MoneySupermarket: www.moneysupermarket.com/mortgages

Motley Fool: www.fool.co.uk/mortgages/compare-mortgages.aspx (an award-winning mortgage service)

4 *Being a smarter saver*

Moneyfacts: www.moneyfacts.co.uk/savings

MoneySavingExpert: www.moneysavingexpert.com/banking

MoneySupermarket: www.moneysupermarket.com/savings

Motley Fool: www.fool.co.uk/savings

National Savings & Investments: www.nsandi.com

5 *Protecting yourself and your assets*

Association of Medical Insurance Intermediaries: www.amii.org.uk

British Insurance Brokers' Association: www.biba.org.uk/ConsumerHome.aspx (find a broker via BIBA)

LifeSearch: www.lifesearch.co.uk (an award-winning life insurance and protection adviser)

Medibroker: www.medibroker.co.uk (a top broker for health and medical insurance)

Moneyfacts: www.moneyfacts.co.uk/insurance

MoneySavingExpert: www.moneysavingexpert.com/insurance

MoneySupermarket: www.moneysupermarket.com/insurance

Motley Fool: www.fool.co.uk/insurance

The AA: www.theaa.com (the UK's biggest insurance broker)

Other leading insurance comparison websites: www.confused.com, www.comparethemarket.com, www.gocompare.com and www.onlyfinance.com/Insurance

Society of Trust and Estate Practitioners: www.step.org (to make a will)

6 *Turning into an intelligent investor*

Discount brokers: www.bestinvest.co.uk, www.cavendishonline.co.uk, www.chartwell-investment.co.uk, www.chelseafs.co.uk, www.fundsnetwork.co.uk, www.h-l.co.uk and www.tqonline.co.uk

Financial Times: www.ft.com (the best newspaper for investors and business people)

Interactive Investor: www.iii.co.uk

London Stock Exchange: www.londonstockexchange.com (Europe's largest stock market)

Money Made Clear: www.moneymadeclear.fsa.gov.uk (advice from the FSA)

Money Week: www.moneyweek.com (the online version of the popular investment magazine)

MoneyExtra: www.moneyextra.com

Moneyfacts: www.moneyfacts.co.uk/investments

MoneySupermarket: www.moneysupermarket.com/shares (search engine to find cheap stockbrokers)

Motley Fool: www.fool.co.uk/investments (my favourite website for investing guidance)

TrustNet: www.trustnet.com (information and research covering investment funds)

7 *Pumping up your pension*

Department for Work and Pensions: www.dwp.gov.uk

Hargreaves Lansdown: www.h-l.co.uk (a leading provider of pensions, annuities and investments)

Moneyfacts: www.moneyfacts.co.uk/pensions

MoneySupermarket: www.moneysupermarket.com/pensions

Motley Fool: www.fool.co.uk/pensions

Pensions calculator: www.pensioncalculator.org (a tool to work out how much retirement income you might receive)

The Pension Service: www.thepensionservice.gov.uk

The Pensions Advisory Service: www.pensionsadvisoryservice.org.uk (free advice from an independent, non-profit organisation)

8 *Steering clear of scams*

Consumer Direct: www.consumerdirect.gov.uk/watch_out/scams

Money Made Clear: www.moneymadeclear.fsa.gov.uk/scams (consumer advice from the FSA)

Office of Fair Trading: www.oft.gov.uk/Consumer/Scams/default.htm

Check to see if a firm is registered with the Financial Services Authority: www.fsa.gov.uk/register

Advice on safe banking online: www.banksafeonline.org.uk and
www.getsafeonline.org

Spotting timeshare scams: www.timeshare.org.uk/scams.html

More on scams at: www.crimes-of-persuasion.com

Index

FINANCIAL TIMES

Think big for less

FT.com

Try the FT for 4 weeks for only £1

In a world shaped by business, the opportunities are endless – especially when you're armed with the right information. That's why the FT is indispensable. Try the FT for 4 weeks for only £1, either delivered direct to your door or with vouchers you can redeem at your local newsagent.*

Take your trial today by calling 0800 298 4709 and quoting 'Book Trial 1' or visit www.ft.com/booktrial1

*This offer applies to customers in the UK only. For subscription offers in other countries please visit www.ft.com/international or call +44 20 7775 6000

We live in **FINANCIAL TIMES**®